# Master of the Midcentury
## The Architecture of William F. Cody

# Master of the Midcentury
# The Architecture of William F. Cody

**Catherine Cody, Jo Lauria, Don Choi**

Foreword by Wim de Wit

PALM SPRINGS
**PRESERVATION**
FOUNDATION

Library of Congress Control Number: 2020949997

ISBN 978-1-58093-530-2

10 9 8 7 6 5 4 3 2

Printed in China

Design by Andrew Byrom

Monacelli, A Phaidon Company
65 Bleecker Street
New York, New York 10012

www.monacellipress.com

William F. Cody, c. 1964.

# Table of contents

10     **Preface**
Catherine Cody

12     **Foreword**
Wim de Wit

18     **Introduction**
*William F. Cody and the Realm of Postwar Modernism*
Don Choi

       **Featured Projects**

34     Del Marcos Apartment Hotel, Palm Springs, California, 1947

38     Dorothy Levin Residence, Palm Springs, California, 1947

44     Haines Studio and Offices, Beverly Hills, California, 1949

48     Thunderbird Country Club Clubhouse and Master Plan, Rancho Mirage, California, 1950

52     William F. and Wini Cody Residence, Palm Springs, California, 1952

60     L'Horizon Hotel, Palm Springs, California, 1952

64     H. Austin Peterson-Frank Sinatra Residence, Rancho Mirage, California, 1953

66     Mission Valley Country Club and Hotel, San Diego, California, 1954

72     Earle E. Jorgensen Residence, Rancho Mirage, California, 1955

78     Villa Real Golfotel, Havana, Cuba, 1955 (unbuilt)

82     The Springs, Palm Springs, California, 1956

90     Edificio Mateal, Havana, Cuba, 1956 (unbuilt)

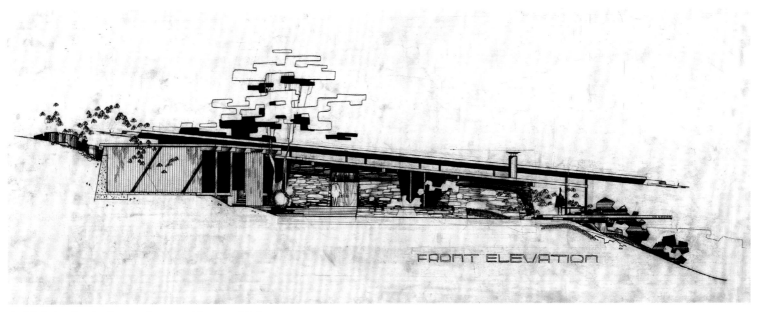

Cody's design drawing for an unknown residence, undated.

92      Eldorado Golf Club Estates Cottages East and West, Indian Wells, California, 1958, 1961

98      Eldorado Country Club Clubhouse, Indian Wells, California, 1959

108     Palm Springs Spa, Palm Springs, California, 1959

116     Racquet Club Cottages West, Palm Springs, California, 1960

122     Louise Durham Nicoletti Residence, Rancho Mirage, California, 1961

128     Palo Alto Hills Golf & Country Club, Palo Alto, California, 1961

130     W. & J. Sloane Company Display House, La Quinta, California, 1961

136     Robert and Betty Cannon Residence, Indian Wells, California, 1961

142     Desert Bel Air Estates, Indian Wells, California, 1961–64

148     Douglas Driggs Residence, Paradise Valley, Arizona, 1962

152     Southridge Inc. Display House (Goldberg Residence), Palm Springs, California, 1962

158     Western Savings & Loan, Tempe, Arizona, 1962

162     Palm Springs Spa Hotel, Palm Springs, California, 1963

170     Jennings B. and Anna Shamel Residence, Indian Wells, California, 1963

178     James and Helen Abernathy Residence, Palm Springs, California, 1963

184     Palm Springs Tennis Club Projects, Palm Springs, California, 1963–73

188     Western Savings & Loan Home Office, Phoenix, Arizona, 1964

192     Valley Wide Center Master Plan, Palm Desert, California, 1964 (unbuilt)

194     Weir McDonald Residence, Paradise Valley, Arizona, 1965

200     Dr. Branch and Carol Kerfoot Residence, Newport Beach, California, 1967

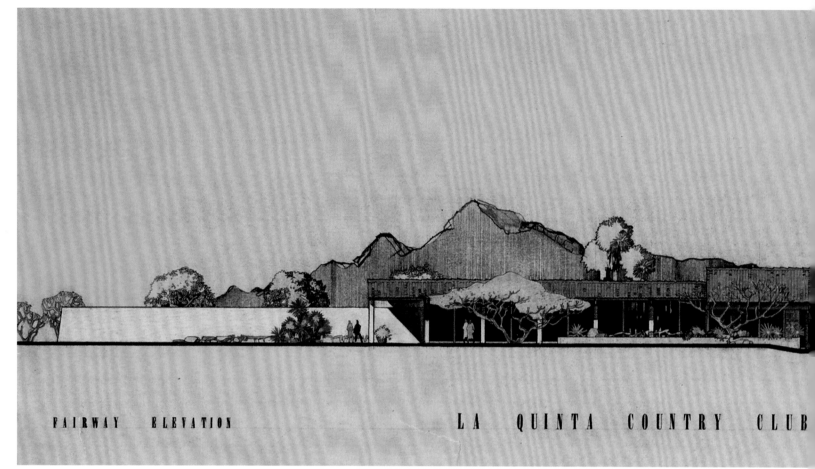

FAIRWAY ELEVATION            LA QUINTA COUNTRY CLUB

Presentation drawing by Cody for La Quinta Country Club, 1964 (unbuilt).

208    Rhu House, Lemurian Fellowship, Ramona, California , 1968

214    St. Theresa Catholic Church, Palm Springs, California, 1968

222    McCulloch Plaza/McCulloch Oil Corporation Headquarters, Los Angeles, California, 1969 (unbuilt)

224    California State University, San Bernardino Library, Audio-Visual and Classroom Building,
       San Bernardino, California , 1971

228    Samuel and Gladys Rubinstein Residence, Rancho Mirage, California, 1972

236    Andreas Hills and Whitewater Country Club, Palm Springs, California, 1972–75

242    Palm Springs Public Library, Palm Springs, California, 1975

246    **William F. Cody Projects**

266    *My Father, William F. Cody*
       Catherine Cody

WILLIAM F. CODY, A.I.A., ARCHITECT

274     **Biographical Timeline**

286     ***William Cody's Artistic Development***
          Jo Lauria and Catherine Cody

292     ***William Cody's Early Work Before Licensure***
          Don Choi and Catherine Cody

300     **Awards and Recognition**

302     **Selected Bibliography**

308     **Acknowledgments**

310     **Contributors**

311     **Credits**

# Preface

Catherine Cody

Forty-five years ago my father asked me to help him write his autobiography. Within a few years, before we could get far along, he had passed away. So without the presence of his voice, and after a very long journey, we are pleased to present the book you now hold. Many other contributions and avenues of research contributed to its development. The first and most important resource has been all the people who knew William F. Cody: the Cody family—especially my sister Lynne and beloved Uncle John Cody, but also numerous colleagues, clients, and friends of Bill Cody who shared their memories of knowing him personally and professionally. Some of their memories are included in this book to introduce the person behind his architectural legacy.

After my eldest sister, Diane, passed away in 2006, I inherited the remainder of my father's papers that had been in a storage unit for decades. My mother, Wini, had made a significant donation of my father's professional archives to Special Collections and Archives at the Kennedy Library, California Polytechnic State University, San Luis Obispo (Cal Poly) in 1978. After my mother's gift, my sister Lynne and I donated the balance of our father's documents. The archives now contain the William F. Cody papers in two separate collections; the cataloging of all the papers presented the opportunity to begin writing my

father's story. Additionally, the Palm Springs Historical Society holds important materials relevant to Bill Cody's life and career, and I knew this endeavor would require a great deal of further research to assemble a comprehensive narrative.

The collaborations necessary to fulfill such an ambitious biographical project began to come together in 2007 when my friend Charles Hollis Jones told me, "You need to meet Jo Lauria. She makes things happen." Soon afterward, I met Jo, a museum curator and design scholar. When I showed Jo the original drawings of Bill Cody, she expressed a strong interest in my concept of a book to honor my father's professional design and architecture career. In addition, working in tandem, we wanted to celebrate Bill Cody's life by organizing a centennial tribute exhibition honoring his architectural design legacy.

When we were seeking a venue for the show, Jo graciously introduced the proposal to the then-director of the Architecture and Design Museum (A+D) in Los Angeles, Tibbie Dunbar, who embraced it. After Tibbie moved on to other pursuits, Jo stepped in as interim executive director of A+D Museum. Together we assembled a curatorial team to oversee the exhibition consisting of myself, Jo as organizing curator, and architecture historians Emily Bills and Don Choi, each

Bill Cody with daughters Lynne, Cathy, and Diane plus Beau the collie.

*Fast Forward: The Architecture of William F. Cody* at A+D Museum, Los Angeles, 2016.

of whom brought their expertise to the project and made significant contributions to the development and execution of the exhibition.

Cal Poly's Special Collections and Archives department director Jessica Holada and department specialist Laura Sorvetti graciously provided information and made available the resources requested for the exhibition. On July 10, 2016 the exhibition *Fast Forward: The Architecture of William F. Cody* opened. Aside from the models, drawings, photographs, and other materials that represented Cody's architectural legacy, a selection of objects and drawings created by Don Choi's design students were included in the exhibition, representing modern-day interpretations of his work. This contemporary reimagining enlivened Cody's vision from the previous century. Andrew Byrom brilliantly translated the concept of the exhibition with his graphic design.

The show traveled to an additional venue beyond the A+D Museum; with the help of Julie Warren, Library Services and Public Relations Manager for the Palm Springs Central Library, it appeared during Palm Springs Modernism Week in 2017. I am very grateful to Jo and Julie for coordinating the exhibition in our family's hometown, in the library that my father designed.

So we continued onward. The exhibition launched the serious work of organizing the book, which now required the support of a publisher. Jo facilitated the introduction to Monacelli, and we worked in partnership to bring this book to fruition. This partnership expanded when we invited our previous collaborator on the exhibition, professor Don Choi, to contribute his expertise on modern architecture and Cody's place in that history. Don's cogent introduction surveying Cody's career within the evolution of midcentury modernism expertly contextualizes the featured projects in the book. Andrew Byrom's book design carries over key ideas from the original exhibition and presents an engaging format throughout. Our research formed the basis of many of these project entries, distilling personal and professional details found in the Cody archives.

I am forever indebted to this team for their contributions to the publication. The book is by far the most comprehensive record to date of my father's architecture and design legacy, as well as an in-depth exploration of his spirit and generosity. I hope it inspires future designers and scholars to further investigate the remarkable achievements of William F. Cody.

# Foreword

## Wim de Wit

The name and work of Palm Springs architect William F. Cody were well-known to me before 2007, when I first met his daughter, Catherine, who wanted to show me the part of her father's archive that was still in the care of the family. While it should not have come as a surprise, considering the architect's attention to detail in his built oeuvre, I was delighted to see the great lengths to which Cody and the draftsmen in his office had gone to produce high-quality renderings and working drawings. As head of the Getty Research Institute's Department of Architecture and Contemporary Art and preparing an exhibition that I cocurated, *Overdrive: L.A. Constructs the Future, 1940–1990* (2013), I was always looking for materials to add to the show and the collections. Cody's work would certainly have been an excellent addition to the Getty's collections, but when I discovered that a large part of his architectural archive was already preserved in the Special Collections and Archives at California Polytechnic State University's Robert E. Kennedy Library in San Luis Obispo, I had to admit that it would make much more sense if the drawings that were still in the hands of the family were housed with the rest of Cody's work. I recommended to Cathy and her relatives that they should make this happen.

This episode did not bring my connection to the Codys to an end. I continued to study their father's ingenious designs, and in early 2012 I was invited to speak at the unveiling of Cody's well-deserved star in Palm Springs Walk of Stars near the Palm Springs Art Museum's Architecture and Design Center. And I continue to be interested in the work of this versatile architect to this day.

One of the aspects that always intrigued me is that, among all the architects who helped promote postwar modernism in Palm Springs, William Cody, a native of Dayton, Ohio, probably felt more at home with the lifestyle of that desert town than anyone else. Charismatic, full of joie de vivre, and, according to numerous accounts, an organizer of great parties, Cody understood what brought people from all over the country to the Coachella Valley: warm weather, the beautiful natural environment, golf courses, tennis courts, clubs for meeting friends and making new business connections, and comfortable houses in which to relax and entertain. Potential clients recognized that Cody genuinely appreciated these qualities of the region, and that he was able to deliver.

Cody's career could thus take off pretty quickly after he arrived in Palm Springs in 1946. The fast-growing town and surrounding communities were in need of many public and private structures and provided work to a host of architects, all of whom were able to develop their own specializations. Los Angeles architect William Krisel, for example, found a niche in designing modular homes, and E. Stewart Williams became the architect to bankers, businessmen, and educational institutions.

Eldorado Country Club, Indian Wells, California, 1959.

For his part, Cody flourished as the architect hired to design clubhouses for country clubs, houses along the fairways of their golf courses, resort hotels, spas, and restaurants. He became so well-known as a designer of these building types that he was offered similar commissions in many other parts of California (Alamo, Malibu, Napa, Palo Alto, and San Diego), elsewhere in the country (El Paso, Texas, and Rapid City, South Dakota), and even abroad (Havana, Cuba and Monterrey, Mexico).

The most elegant, in my opinion, and most famous of all his buildings as far as the projection of the Palm Springs lifestyle was concerned is the clubhouse for the Eldorado Country Club in Indian Wells (1959). Seamlessly combining practical and aesthetic elements, Cody designed a spacious glass-and-brick building that was slightly elevated above the golf course and pond. This raised position allowed, on the one hand, for the construction of an underground parking facility for golf carts. At the same time, it gave the building, with its deep porch, well-proportioned

concrete columns, and glass-enclosed cella, a sense of monumentality and calm that drew its inspiration from that ur-example of Western architecture: the Greek temple.

In this respect, the clubhouse seems related stylistically to the work of the great German architect Ludwig Mies van der Rohe, even though Mies's building to which it seems most closely linked, the New National Gallery in Berlin (1968) was not conceptualized, designed, and constructed until years after the Eldorado Clubhouse had been completed. Temples and museums, however, are introverted, focused as they are on the celebration of the god or art inside. In contrast, the Eldorado Country Clubhouse is designed in its totality to look out toward the surrounding environment: the green lawns, statuesque palm trees, and gorgeous colors of the Santa Rosa Mountains. Viewed from the outside, the clubhouse looks like a graceful temple well-integrated in the landscape, while from the inside, with all its amenities intended to pamper the members, it is almost more

Shamel Residence, Indian Wells, California, 1963.

Palm Springs Spa, Palm Springs, California, 1959.

like a view camera from which one observes a natural panorama.

Cody's design philosophy, directed at integrating his buildings into the landscape and making the borders between nature and architecture as minimal as possible, was typical of many Southern California, midcentury modern architects. His training at the University of Southern California had prepared him well for this approach to residential design. Yet, Cody was not the kind of architect who developed one stylistic approach and stayed with it for the rest of his career. On the contrary, working closely with his clients, he chose the building materials and forms that went best with the client's budget and brief, on the one hand, and his own design concept and sense of aesthetics, on the other. We therefore see in Cody's oeuvre residences with a structural system not only in wood, but also in steel, as in the Shamel Residence (1963); office buildings in steel (the Western Savings & Loan office in Phoenix, Arizona, 1963) or concrete (the branch office of the same bank in Tempe, 1964); and structures in lightweight concrete (Palm Springs Spa arcade, 1959). St. Theresa Church in Palm Springs (1968), built primarily in wood with some details in steel and with external walls of concrete, is an especially good example of Cody's versatility in the use of materials.

In all these projects, Cody was able to produce decidedly modernist designs. He even was able to pursue this stylistic methodology when one of his clients, Mrs. Gladys Rubinstein, told him she wanted a house resembling a Mexican hacienda. His design for this residence is a true mixture of a Southern California post-and-beam house and a Latin American house with heavy, stuccoed walls and terra-cotta roofs. In spite of the closed walls, Cody was able to maintain the relationship with nature by including a central courtyard and patios that at all times provide vistas to the surroundings. The house could easily have felt like a closed-off monastery keeping the outside world at bay and overprotecting the inside, but the blind front wall is just a ploy. Inside no one ever has to wonder where they are vis-à-vis the country club or the mountains.

It is hard to imagine where Cody would have taken his design work if his career had not been cut short. Would he have continued to design Southern California midcentury modern houses, or would he have further developed the use of Brutalist elements as he had done in the Palm Springs Public Library (1975), or would he have left the residential-design world altogether to take on commissions from corporations, as he had been doing since the mid-1960s with California entrepreneur Robert P. McCulloch? We will never know. For most architects, success comes late in life. Cody, who died in 1978 at the relatively young age of 62, tragically never reached this stage.

Palm Springs Library, Palm Springs, California, 1975.

Rubenstein Residence, Rancho Mirage, California, 1972.

But success had definitely not escaped him. William Cody produced more than five hundred designs (built and unbuilt) during a career of about thirty years, which is a stunningly high number. Many of his houses are still standing and are attracting younger generations of buyers. Cody's original design concepts—characterized by direct interaction between man-made and natural environments, and stunning views across fairways, the desert, or toward the mountains—are today appreciated just as much as they were in the 1950s and '60s. The many awards offered to Cody throughout his professional career testify to the recognition and appreciation he received from his peers and clients alike. That Cody's name will continue to be known for many generations to come, not just on a star in the Palm Springs Walk of Stars, nor even due to the publication of this book, is seen in how his architecture has left a lasting impact on the built environment of Southern California—and beyond.

St. Theresa Catholic Church, Palm Springs, California, 1968.

Cody's presentation drawing for the proposed mountain terminal of the Mt. San Jacinto tramway.

WINTER PARK AUTHORITY

SPRINGS · PHOENIX · LOS ANGELES ·

# Introduction: *William F. Cody and the Realm of Postwar Modernism*

Don Choi

Of all the architects described as desert modernists, William F. Cody (1916–1978) is probably the one whose accomplishments most exceed his personal fame. A designer of true talent and imagination, during an independent career of only about a quarter of a century he created works remarkable for their range and quality. Although primarily known as a Palm Springs architect, he completed dozens of projects outside the Coachella Valley–in Los Angeles, San Diego, and the San Francisco Bay Area, not to mention Arizona, Colorado, and Texas. He also designed for sites in Mexico, Honduras, and Cuba, suggesting that the term *desert modernist* fails to capture the full extent of his oeuvre. Compared to his colleagues and rivals in the Palm Springs area, Cody distinguished himself through an exceptionally wide palette of materials and approaches. During any given year, he was likely to be working on projects of widely divergent functions and styles. For example, in 1955, he was mapping out the angular, wood-and-stone Springs restaurant in Palm Springs as well as a rectilinear reinforced-concrete office building for Havana; in 1958, he was designing the serenely refined Eldorado Country Club in Indian Wells but also working on the slickly commercial Hi Fidelity Unlimited store in Menlo Park (fig. 1–4). As a highly original modernist active in multiple regions with a broad range of clients and programs, Cody's work illuminates the broader state of architecture from the immediate postwar era through the early 1970s.

For modernist architects, the 1950s were a time of both crisis and triumph. Back in 1932, Philip Johnson and Henry-Russell Hitchcock's famous exhibition at New York's Museum of Modern Art, *Modern Architecture: International Exhibition,* had promoted the idea of the International Style–a "unified and inclusive" style that "exists throughout the world." They singled out the Swiss-French architect Le Corbusier, writing that, "his name has become almost synonymous with the new architecture."[1] By the 1950s, though, the orthodox modernism championed by Le Corbusier and the group he cofounded–CIAM (Congrès Internationaux d'Architecture Moderne)–had begun to splinter amid ideological disagreements, ultimately resulting in the dissolution of CIAM in 1959. To some observers, this marked the end of a golden age when the principles of modernist architecture appeared inviolable and inevitable. Writing in 1966, Hitchcock stated, "Who shall say, a generation after its heyday, when the International Style died? That it is over is today as clear as that the near-revolution it constituted remains the basis … of later modern architecture."[2]

From another perspective, though, this lack of orthodoxy was simply the consequence of the flourishing of modernism outside its birthplace in Western Europe. In the United States, for example, the corporate modernism of buildings such as Skidmore, Owings & Merrill's Lever House in New York soon

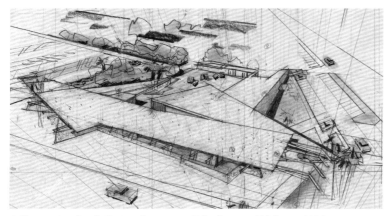

**1:** Perspective sketch, Springs Restaurant, Palm Springs, California, 1956.

**3:** View of clubhouse from southeast, Eldorado Country Club, Indian Wells, California, 1959.

**2:** Drawing, Edificio Mateal, Havana, Cuba (unbuilt; designed 1956).

**4:** Presentation drawing, Hi Fidelity Unlimited, Menlo Park (unbuilt; designed 1958).

**5:** View from northeast, Eames House, Pacific Palisades, California. Charles Eames, 1949.

**6:** View of clubhouse from northwest, Eldorado Country Club, Indian Wells, California, 1959.

became a standard for office buildings around the world. In Southern California, the Case Study Houses, including the Eames House of 1949, purported to offer models for accessible modernist houses, while in the San Francisco Bay Area, William Wurster and others designed buildings that seemed to fuse local traditions with International Style influences (fig. 5). Palm Springs, of course, hosted some of the most beautiful and creative of these local developments.

However, the modernist architecture of areas outside major cities was often derided as merely "regional," perhaps interesting but only peripheral to the main line of development. Postwar Palm Springs, a small community with a short history as a city, could stake no claim as a major cultural center. In fact, though, the relative newness and isolation of Palm Springs made it an ideal setting for the development of modernist architecture. Unlike architects in Paris or Berlin or even Chicago, those of Palm Springs were bound neither by traditions of local architecture nor by the desire to reject such traditions. This freedom encouraged Cody and his peers to refine and exploit certain aspects of modernism in ways beyond what earlier European architects had imagined, especially in regard to the natural landscape. As Cody stated, "Good contemporary architecture is a world wide (sic) expression, conditioned by the geographic location, politics and economics of the various

countries throughout the world. Here, on the desert, it should flourish."[3] Indeed, the wealth, freedom, and optimism of postwar Palm Springs created favorable circumstances for Cody and his vision of modernism.

During his career, Cody's works were published in the major architectural journals of the day, including *Architectural Record,* the mainstream standard-bearer, and *Arts & Architecture*, the progressive Los Angeles-based magazine. In addition, three Cody projects were chosen for the twelve-volume Japanese series *World's Contemporary Architecture*, published in Tokyo in 1953. In volume 4, dedicated to American houses, Cody's design for the Dorothy Levin House appeared alongside some of the greatest homes of the century, including the Eames House, Philip Johnson's Glass House, and Frank Lloyd Wright's Fallingwater.[4]

Unfortunately, a debilitating stroke in 1973, when he was only fifty-six, robbed Cody not only of his ability to design but also of his prominence in the historiography of modern architecture. After his death in 1978, critical and popular tastes began to move away from modernism; by the 1990s, when modernism—especially the midcentury modernism that Cody exemplified—began to return to favor, Cody's career had been over for a full generation. In contrast, many of Cody's Palm Springs peers, even those born before him, such as Albert Frey (1903–1998) and E. Stewart

**7:** Aerial view, L'Horizon Hotel, Palm Springs, California, 1952.

**8:** View of townhouses, Lafayette Park, Detroit, Michigan. Ludwig Mies van der Rohe, 1959.

Williams (1909–2005), lived long enough to enjoy a critical and popular rebirth. Although never forgotten by the architectural cognoscenti in Palm Springs, Cody remained underappreciated by scholars and unknown to the wider public. Yet his work deserves attention both for its exceptional architectural qualities and for the light it sheds on the broader themes of modernist architecture.

### Theoretical vs. Applied

Unlike Le Corbusier, Walter Gropius, and many other European architects, modernist designers in California generally showed little interest in crafting broad, theoretical arguments for modern architecture, preferring to deal with the particular circumstances at hand.[5] The Bay Area architect and educator William Wurster made this explicit, stating that in California, "It was fortunate that the climate, the new taste for outdoor living, and an informal society freed clients from rigid preconceptions. It was sensible to base the design on the kind of life people wanted, and *not* on the basis of theoretical modernism."[6] Geographically and culturally removed from interwar Europe, Wurster found the polemic statements of Le Corbusier and other designers to be of little relevance for his own circumstances. In his influential essays in *Toward an Architecture* (1923), Le Corbusier famously posed the dyad "architecture or revolution," arguing that modern architecture was necessary to stave off social catastrophe. But in the warmth and burgeoning wealth of postwar California, such ominous statements must have seemed no more than distant fantasies.

The belief in the practical and in everyday life, rather than in grand theoretical claims, certainly characterized

the American-born architects of postwar Palm Springs.[7] Cody wrote no exhortatory manifestos and made no claims for the revolutionary potential of his designs. Like his Palm Springs peers, he preferred building over writing, and flesh-and-blood clients over an abstract audience or school of thought. His statements about architecture were embodied in his designs, and he celebrated the ability of his field to support a new vision of American society. As Palm Springs began to attract a broader population of visitors and residents after World War II, Cody's work was instrumental in developing the image of the city as a place of leisure and recreation, a stark contrast to the original context of modernist architecture in interwar Europe. He wrote, "Architecture … set free by the principles of new creative thinking is developing, in our era, an identity reflecting man's greatest period of affluence."[8]

One of the manifestations of this wealth was of course the country club, which had boomed in the 1920s and then declined during the 1930s and wartime years. In the postwar revival of country clubs, Cody was one of the first architects to design modernist clubhouses, and, perhaps more important, contributed to a new model of development. At Thunderbird Country Club, he suggested to developer Johnny Dawson and golf course designer Lawrence Hughes that residential lots be planned along the course with no obstructions between house and fairway; *Palm Springs Life* magazine boasted, "this new concept of fairway living was born in Palm Springs and is being imitated by other country clubs throughout the country."[9] At Eldorado Country Club in Indian Wells, Cody completed a 53,000-square-foot clubhouse in 1959; according to an Eldorado advertisement,

**9:** Entrance, Springs Restaurant, Palm Springs, California, 1956.

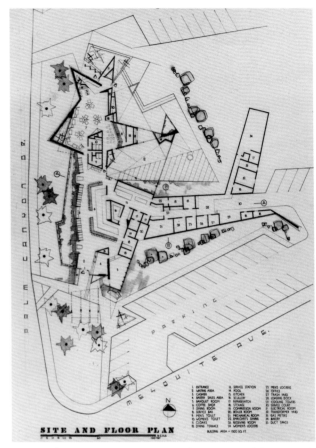

**10:** Plan drawing, Springs Restaurant, Palm Springs, California, 1956.

"Gentleman Gene Sarazen likened it to the Palace at Versailles. Other notables have called it 'The Taj Mahal of the Desert.'"[10] At any rate, such was the prestige of the club that it hosted the Ryder Cup in 1959 and welcomed former president Eisenhower as a winter guest and honorary club member in 1961.

Cody's elegant clubhouse design announced Eldorado as an unequivocally modern setting for golf and socializing (fig. 6). Looking out over perfect greens from its brilliant white veranda, the Santa Rosa Mountains looming in the distance, its wealthy visitors must have felt that they had entered a kind of modern paradise, an oasis of leisure in the midst of the desert. Along the fairways, the Shamel Residence (1963), Cannon Residence (1961), and other Cody-designed homes shared in this vision of modern leisure and expansive space.

### Universal vs. Individual

Philip Johnson and Henry-Russell Hitchcock coined the term *International Style* to refer to the modernist architecture arising in various places in the 1920s that appeared to lack national characteristics. Many of the architects they featured in the MoMA exhibition were attempting to find generalizable solutions to architectural problems, such as the lack of housing in interwar European cities. For example, in New Frankfurt, Germany, Ernst May and his colleagues designed about 12,000 new housing units along modernist lines. Similarly, Le Corbusier wrote, "We must create a mass-production state of mind. A state of mind for building mass-production housing," and many of his seminal works of the 1920s were intended as models for such endeavors.[11]

In contrast, even compared to some of his California peers, Cody had comparatively little interest in designing prototypical structures.[12] For example, his close friend A. Quincy Jones, in partnership with Frederick Emmons, produced several designs for Joseph Eichler that became the models for thousands of executed Eichler homes. William Krisel's legacy largely derives from prototypical designs that served as the basis for thousands of homes in tract developments in Palm Springs and elsewhere. Cody, though, saw each project as an opportunity to address particular circumstances. On occasion he designed multiunit developments with standardized plans, but he still created variety through site planning and subtle variations. For example, rather than being lined up in rows, the propeller-shaped units of L'Horizon Hotel (1952) are irregularly placed to secure views and ensure privacy (fig. 7). Mainstream modernist planning emphasized just the type of repetition and rectilinearity Cody sought to avoid, as seen for instance in Lafayette

**11:** Dining nook with exterior sun shade, Springs Restaurant, Palm Springs, California, 1956.

**13:** Presentation drawing, St. Theresa Church, Palm Springs, California, 1968.

**12:** Presentation drawing, Villa Real Golfotel, Havana, Cuba (unbuilt; designed 1955).

Park (1956–59) in Detroit by Ludwig Hilbersheimer and Mies van der Rohe (fig. 8).

The layout of L'Horizon Hotel also shows that Cody was as comfortable working with free angles as he was with the conventional rectangular grid so typical to modernism. Few right angles are to be seen in The Springs restaurant (1956) in Palm Springs, one of Cody's most dynamic designs. With its zigzag plan and sharply angled motifs, this project offers an eye-pleasing alternative to the gaudy Googie style that was

flourishing in Los Angeles, especially in the restaurants designed by Armet & Davis (fig. 9–10). That Cody knew and appreciated this kind of architecture was no surprise, though–Eldon Davis of Armet & Davis was a USC classmate and a lifelong friend. The brio and exuberance of The Springs might have differed from the restrained elegance of many of Cody's other works, but even here, Cody's eye for elegance is on display (fig. 11). For other projects, he used angles to fit a building into the contours of its site; a 1955 rendering shows the Villa Real Golfotel in Havana located on top

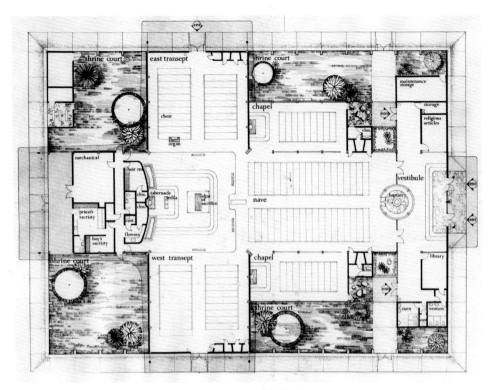

14: Plan drawing, St. Theresa Church, Palm Springs, Palm Springs, California, 1968.

15: View of crossing from west, St. Theresa Church, Palm Springs, California, 1968.

of a gentle hill, its arms reaching down the slopes into the landscape (fig. 12).

The design for St. Theresa Catholic Church in Palm Springs was perhaps Cody's most personally important commission (fig. 13). Completed in 1968, this project was the capstone of Cody's career, demonstrating how his modernist principles could produce a profoundly spiritual space. He designed everything from the site plan down to the furniture— with additional artwork provided by other designers, including stained glass by Jos Maes of Laguna Beach and some ritual furnishings by Barnabas Wasson of Yarnell, Arizona. As a modernist, Cody detested the unthinking use of historical motifs, complaining, "It is sickening that we are plagued with pseudo Roman medal-stamp (sic) columns, large imitation wine jugs and Grecian villas and neo (and sub-neo) classic design better fitted for a Hollywood back-lot 'B' picture."[13] Yet he also believed in the value of the past, noting, "we must realize the past has always influenced architecture in every era of man's existence."[14] He knew that much of the power of a church building lay in its position within a long history of religious architecture, and that a church not recognizable as a church would lose much of its meaning.

For the plan of St. Theresa, Cody adopted a conventional cruciform layout with a broad nave, a transept, and aisles (fig. 14). Over the crossing, glulam beams sweep upward to frame a square skylight; although original in execution, the effect parallels that of the domes and lanterns of historical Catholic churches, for instance St. Peter's Basilica in the Vatican (fig. 15). In the nave and aisles, the placement of the clerestory windows prevent distracting views into the immediate environment but allow vistas of sky and mountains, making the interior feel sheltered but not constrained. Although more often associated with steel and glass, in this church Cody showed his love of wood, as found in the graceful, unadorned pews as well as in the contours and cutouts of the structural elements (fig. 16). For the travertine altars and baptismal font, Cody chose simple shapes that emphasize the texture and color of the stone (fig. 17). Unable to find an American artisan willing to attempt the slender span of the altars, he ultimately contracted with Italian manufacturer Sicea Marmi.

**Nature**

Critics often targeted what they saw as the industrial, impersonal qualities of modernist houses. Frank Lloyd Wright, a trenchant critic of almost all architecture except his own, once declared, "most 'new' modernist houses manage to look as though cut from cardboard with scissors, the sheets of cardboard folded or bent in rectangles. . . . The cardboard forms thus made are glued together in box-like forms—in a childish

**16:** Pews, St. Theresa Church, Palm Springs, California, 1968.

**17:** Baptismal font, St. Theresa Church, Palm Springs, California, 1968.

attempt to make buildings resemble steamships, flying machines, or locomotives."[15] Le Corbusier's iconic Villa Savoye (1931), for example, stands within a clearing in the woods, safely set off from any encroaching vegetation. Its abstract, white surfaces and stark geometric form remove it from the realm of nature.

Cody preferred that his buildings engage nature more directly. The Shamel Residence, for example, incorporated nature in many ways. At the entry, a shallow pool extended from outside to inside, connecting the exterior to a spacious atrium open to the sky. Inside, planters and small rectangular gardens dotted the plan. From the living room at the back of the house, residents would have looked out over a garden and the pool to the green of the golf course and to the mountains beyond (fig. 18).

Water was particularly important in the desert environment of the Coachella Valley, and Cody often introduced swimming pools, reflecting pools, fountains, and other water features to his projects. One of the most memorable was the 150-foot-long pool that bordered the entry arcade of the Palm Springs Spa Bathhouse (1959); lined in Italian glass tile, this glittering feature cast dappled reflections on the underside of the arcade's shallow domes, creating a sense of play that complemented the arcade's starkly refined lines (fig. 19). Even the humble residential

shower attracted Cody's attention; for example, the glass shower stall of the Perlberg Residence (1952) in Palm Springs opens to a small courtyard, connecting this confined space with greenery and the sky (fig. 20).

**Transparency and Lightness**

The close relationship with nature in Cody's designs was intertwined with his pursuit of transparency and lightness—qualities fundamental to the modernist reaction against historical masonry structures. As Alfred Barr had noted in the catalog for the 1932 International Style exhibition, "the modern architect working in the new style conceives of his building not as a structure of brick or masonry with thick columns and supporting walls resting heavily on the earth but rather as a skeleton enclosed by a thin light shell."[16] However, in many of the early works of the European modernists, this desire for thinness and openness worked better in theory than in practice. Le Corbusier's Villa Savoye was notoriously uncomfortable—the expansive areas of glass that created transparency also guaranteed staggering heat loss in the cool climate of suburban Paris. In contrast, the warmth of Palm Springs—not to mention cheap energy to power air-conditioning and heating systems—allowed transparency with little regret.

In the Shamel Residence, as well as most of his other house designs, Cody used sliding glass doors

**18:** View toward golf course, Shamel Residence, Indian Wells, California, 1963.

**19:** View of entry arcade, Palm Springs Spa, Palm Springs, California, 1959.

**21:** Plan drawing, Shamel Residence, Indian Wells, California, 1963.

**20:** View of shower and shower court, Perlberg Residence,
Palm Springs, California, 1952.

**22:** Interior, Eames House, Pacific Palisades. Charles Eames, 1949.

**23:** View of carport from southeast, Cody Residence, Palm Springs, California, 1952.

that allowed easy access to outdoor terraces and pools and also pulled in the dramatic scenery of the Coachella Valley (fig. 21). This house was based on a simple 12-by-12-foot structural grid of 4-by-4-inch steel columns that allowed extreme flexibility in planning. Instead of pursuing the universal, undifferentiated space preferred by Ludwig Mies van der Rohe, though, Cody used the grid as a framework for a rich variety of spaces. Some of the 12-by-12-foot spatial units were completely open, while others were bounded by walls of glass or even stone; some were roofed, others were open to the sky. The floor of a square might be carpet, flagstone, terrazzo, garden, or pool. As *Architectural Record* noted of the house, "its design reflects the infinite variety of life that takes place in a house of this kind."[17] In contrast to the work of many other modernists, Cody's transparency and openness did not necessarily entail homogeneity.

### Materials and Structure

The lightness and transparency of modernist architecture in interwar Europe were often compromised by the cost and scarcity of steel. Steel architecture had developed earlier in the United States than in Europe, notably in the skyscrapers of Chicago

in the 1880s. Richard Neutra, who pioneered steel-frame residential construction at the Lovell Health House (1929) in Los Angeles, may have learned about steel construction when he worked for Holabird and Roche in Chicago. In the United States, steel production had boomed during World War II, and once restrictions on civilian use were lifted, California became one of the most fruitful sites for postwar experimentation. For example, the Eames House and many of the other Case Study Houses promoted by *Arts & Architecture* magazine were built in steel (fig. 22). Palm Springs became particularly fertile ground for the development of steel-framed houses, especially after Neutra's sublime design for the home of Edgar Kaufmann in 1947. Cody, in fact, designed an addition to the Kaufmann Residence in 1963 for Joseph and Nelda Linsk, who had purchased it from the Kaufmann estate. Nelda later described Cody as "brilliant," adding that Neutra once visited the house and "said he thought Bill had done a magnificent job" in designing the new office and family room.[18]

Cody used steel frequently and creatively, and the Shamel Residence was recognized with the American Institute of Steel Construction's Architectural Award

**24:** View on entry axis toward pool, Cannon Residence, Indian Wells, California, 1961.

**25:** View from northwest, Farnsworth House, Plano, Illinois. Ludwig Mies van der Rohe, 1951.

**26:** Window detail, Farnsworth House, Plano, Illinois. Ludwig Mies van der Rohe.

of Excellence in 1965. Cody's own house, designed and constructed from 1946 to 1952, serves as a cogent statement of Cody's approach to architecture. Its steel structure is remarkably slender, comprising square columns 3 inches on each side, and tees plus a roof slab that Cody boasted was only 4 inches deep. However, steel was only one element in Cody's palette, and unlike many earlier modernists, he had little interest in promoting an industrial aesthetic. For example, in the Cody Residence the willowy steel columns contrast with the thick, low-tech adobe wall that surrounds the house and with the wood surfaces of the ceiling and walls (fig. 23). In the Cannon Residence, Cody worked on the interiors with furniture designer Maurice Martiné; the result is a building with clean, modernist lines but a richness of color, material, and texture. For example, the squares of the quarry tile floor contrast with the linear redwood siding of the ceiling and with the rubble stonework of the fireplace wall (fig.24). More generally, Cody viewed materials as an artist would, exploiting their distinct qualities to achieve his architectural goals.

### "God is in the details."

When speaking to architecture students at Cal Poly, where his close friend George Hasslein was the founding dean of the College of Architecture and Environmental Design, Cody once noted, "God is in the details."[19] This maxim is most closely associated with Mies van der Rohe, whose modernist steel-and-glass works also boast immaculate architectural details. However, for Mies and Cody, the rationale for these details differed. For Mies, the window details of the Farnsworth House, completed in 1951, expressed the materials and construction of the building (fig. 25). In turn, construction was the basis of both form and meaning: "The few authentic structures of our period exhibit construction as a component of building. Building and meaning are one. The manner of building is decisive and of testimonial significance," he wrote.[20] In other words, the construction detail spoke of the essential nature of the building (fig. 26). For Cody, one telling example is his favored "hush-and-flush" glazing detail, in which panes of glass vanish directly into sill and ceiling without any projecting molding or frame (fig. 27–28). This detail was important to him not so

**27:** Kitchen, Shamel Residence, Indian Wells, California, 1963.

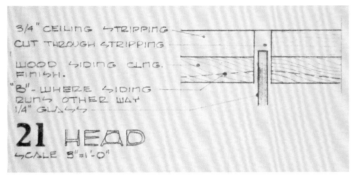

**28:** Glass detail, Shamel Residence, Indian Wells, California, 1963.

**29:** View from north, Shamel Residence, Indian Wells, California, 1963.

much because it expressed the building's materials and construction, but because it allowed the building to disappear—the plane of the roof, for instance, could extend from the ceiling inside to the eaves outside without interruption, framing unobstructed desert views. For Cody, then, the building was less important as an object than as the means for an experience. Mies probably would have objected to the hybrid steel-and-wood structure of the Shamel Residence, feeling that the wooden beams compromised the principles of steel structure. Cody, on the other hand, exploited the steel columns for their slenderness and the wooden beams for their sculptural qualities (fig. 29).

**Functionalism and Minimalism**

Of all of the myths of modernism, perhaps the most deeply seated is that modernist architecture was intended to be functionalist above all; Louis Sullivan's dictum "form ever follows function" has been hauled out—and misinterpreted—as a basis for modern architecture for the past 120 years. Although anything more than a cursory glance at the writings of Le Corbusier or even Walter Gropius should dispel

the notion that modernism was originally imagined to be a simply utilitarian pursuit, it is true that the first generation of modernists generally designed buildings bereft of ornament. This was fundamental to their revolution against the highly ornamented historical styles that they felt were vitiating modern culture. However, even though Cody believed that faux-historical ornament had no place in the clear air and new era of the Coachella Valley, he saw no need to jettison the *concept* of ornament. Like a construction detail, ornament could contribute to his architectural goals. As a modernist, he avoided ornament for its own sake, but he frequently shaped basic architectural or functional elements into expressive forms.

For example, for the bar area of Eldorado Country Club, Cody designed several pendant lamps that differ in size, shape, and material while still showing familial resemblances; as with his architecture in general, these lamps are simple and modern without being simplistic (fig. 30). At The Springs restaurant, the sculpted shape of the projecting beams supplemented the dynamic angles of the plan and elevation (fig. 31).

**30:** Bar and pendant lamps, clubhouse, Eldorado Country Club, Indian Wells, 1959.

**31:** View from southwest toward entry, Springs Restaurant, Palm Springs, California, 1956.

William Cody may have been a modernist, but he was no minimalist. And while his buildings were functional, he understood that the experience of any given building far exceeded its utilitarian roles. The Eldorado clubhouse, for instance, was not simply a collection of places to drink, dress, and socialize—it was an expression of a new kind of life and leisure, and of the unique possibilities of this striking desert environment. Cody's country club architecture appealed in other climes as well: in addition to the Villa Real Golfotel in Havana, he designed Club de Golf Santa Anita and Puerto de Oro Country Club in Guadalajara, Mexico, not to mention many other country club projects in Texas, Arizona, and other California locales (fig. 32).

### The Realm of Modernism
Because of his strong presence in Palm Springs, it is tempting to label Cody as essentially a desert modernist, a regional architect who worked on the periphery in Southern California. Moreover, in 1940, when Cody went to USC, Los Angeles itself was not yet the cultural hub it has since become; it was only the fifth-largest city in the United States by population, less than half the size of Chicago and barely one-fifth as large as New York. Palm Springs was hardly a city at all—the 1940 census recorded only 3,434 residents, and ten years earlier the Census Bureau had not even classified Palm Springs as an urban area. For Cody, though, this environment perfectly suited his desire to create architecture free of the cultural constraints of established metropolitan centers. In the Coachella Valley, Cody could develop modern architecture for its own sake, rather than as a polemical reaction against the European historical styles of the 1800s and early 1900s. He could combine steel and glass

with wood, stone, and adobe without fearing that he would be deemed insufficiently revolutionary. He could fully exploit the transparency and lightness of modern architecture without worrying about heat loss or the scarcity of steel (at least after wartime restrictions were lifted). If modernist architecture was rooted in freedom from convention, then Cody's work was modernist to the core, neither encumbered by the historical styles of the past nor limited by the doctrines of earlier modernist designers. In this way, William Cody did not merely occupy a marginal place in the realm of modernist architecture. Instead, he showed how a geographically and culturally isolated place could support the full flowering of modernist ideals.

**32:** Presentation drawing, Club de Golf Santa Anita Country Club, Guadalajara, Mexico, 1974.

**Footnotes**

**1.** Henry-Russell Hitchcock and Philip Johnson, *The International Style* (New York: W. W. Norton & Company, 1966), 19.

**2.** Ibid, xi.

**3.** J. M. F. Taylor, "William F. Cody A.I.A: A Comment on Architecture," *Palm Springs Life*, August 1964: 32.

**4.** Cody and Wright shared a client, the oilman and geophysicist John Gillin, who had houses underway from both architects at the same time. Wright's design for Gillin's Dallas house was commissioned in 1950, but construction continued until after Wright's death in 1959. Gillin commissioned Cody in 1957 for a house at Thunderbird Country Club in Rancho Mirage.

**5.** Richard Neutra was a major exception, but although he made his career in California, he was born and educated in Vienna.

**6.** William Wurster, "The Twentieth-Century Architect," in *Architecture: A Profession and a Career* (Washington, DC: The American Institute of Architects, 1945): 9.

**7.** This divide between Californian and European modernists can be seen in Palm Springs as well. Unlike Cody and the U.S.-born Palm Springs architects, Albert Frey, who was born in Switzerland and who trained in Le Corbusier's Paris office, published a book-length manifesto: In Search of a Living Architecture (1939).

**8.** J. M. F. Taylor, 26.

**9.** Bud Taylor, "Crusade Against Mediocrity," *Palm Springs Life, 1960–61 Annual Pictorial*, September 1960: 72.

**10.** Magazine advertisement for Eldorado Country Club, circa 1960s, MS0163, Box 74, Folder 10, Special Collections and Archives, California Polytechnic State University.

**11.** Le Corbusier, *Toward an Architecture*, trans. John Goodman (Los Angeles: Getty Publications, 2007), 88.

**12.** Prior to opening his own office, Cody contributed to the development and popularization of the ranch house through his work for Cliff May. Among other designs, Cody worked on what would become *House Beautiful's* Pace-Setter House, which was built in 1947 and became the focus of the entire February 1948 issue. This house also appeared in the 1950 book *Sunset Western Ranch Houses*, a popular introduction to this new type of residence.

**13.** J. M. F. Taylor, 32.

**14.** Ibid, 28.

**15.** Frank Lloyd Wright, *The Essential Frank Lloyd Wright*, ed. Bruce Brooks Pfeiffer (Princeton: Princeton University Press, 2008): 190.

**16.** Alfred H. Barr, Jr., foreword to *Modern Architecture* (New York: Museum of Modern Art, 1932): 14.

**17.** "Familiar Buildings Win A.I.S.C. Awards," *Architectural Record* 138, no. 10 (1965): 346.

**18.** David Lansing, "Nelda Linsk, Then and Now," *Palm Springs Life*, 1 June 2016. https://www.palmspringslife.com/nelda-linsk-then-and-now/.

**19.** Catherine Cody, email message to the author, February 16, 2019.

**20.** Ludwig Mies van der Rohe, "(With Infinite Slowness Arises the Great Form)," in Joan Ockman and Edward Eigen, eds., *Architecture Culture 1943–1968* (New York: Columbia University, 1993): 164.

# Featured Projects

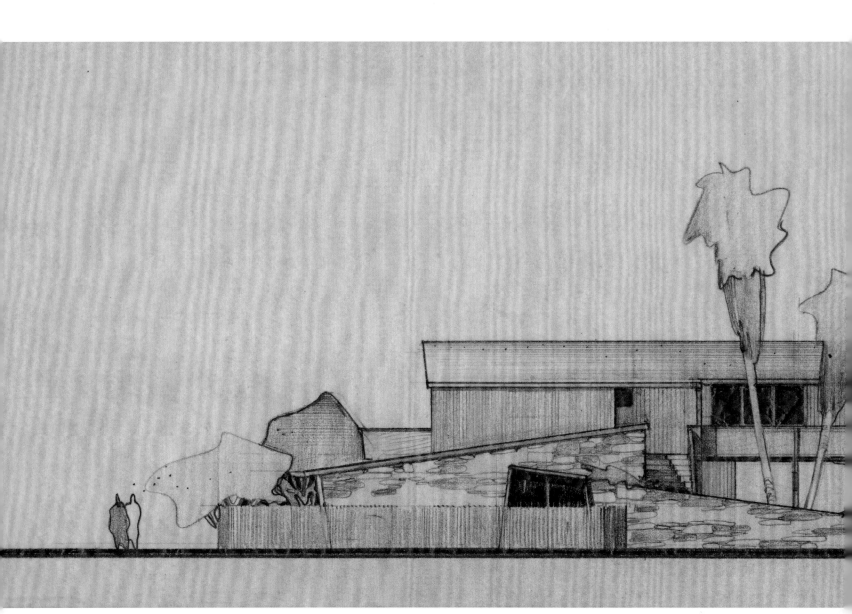

Cody drawing of the north elevation of the Del Marcos Apartment Hotel on Baristo St.

BARISTO ST. ELEVATION

W.F.C.

# Del Marcos Apartment Hotel

Palm Springs | California | 1947

Cody was only thirty-one years old when he designed the Del Marcos Apartment Hotel, a project that brought him international attention. The Del Marcos received attention not only in *Architectural Forum* (July 1949), *House & Garden* (July 1949), and the *Los Angeles Examiner*, among other American publications, but also in the Japanese book *World's Contemporary Architecture*, volume 2 (1953). Even more importantly, this hotel established Cody as one of the founding architects of the Palm Springs postwar boom as a city of promise and leisure. He designed the landscaping as well as the building, while Emily Laser served as interior decorator. Much of the furniture was custom designed, including tables and chairs by Maurice Martiné, who became one of Cody's preferred collaborators.

The Del Marcos was described as an "apartment hotel" in which the rooms were made to feel like living rooms rather than typical hotel rooms; the mattresses and box springs could be partially stowed under the headboards, transforming into sofas. Accommodations ranged from hotel rooms to four-room apartment suites with kitchens, making them convenient for long stays. All rooms boasted views of the central swimming pool, and most of the mountains as well. As *The Desert Sun* wrote upon the hotel's opening, "it is an inside-outside way of living with huge window areas overlooking Palm Springs' wonderful vistas; typical of Architect William Cody's designs." This kind of informal but refined lifestyle became fundamental to the allure of the area as a retreat from Los Angeles and a refuge from cold-climate regions.

The strong abstract forms of the Del Marcos make it a clearly modern building, but its local stone roots it in its desert environment. Like Frank Lloyd Wright at Taliesin West and his son Lloyd Wright at the Joshua Tree Retreat Center, two complexes underway at the same time as the Del Marcos, Cody used rough, irregular stone in angled walls that mimic the desert mountains. These angles appear also in a door on the main facade and in the stairs. Behind the stone walls, wood is the dominant material, used as both structure and siding. The overall effect is both rustic and refined, a compelling combination for the setting and function.

Cody's landscape design included desert plants such as ocotillo and barrel cactus.

View from the north, showing the breezeway leading to the pool patio.

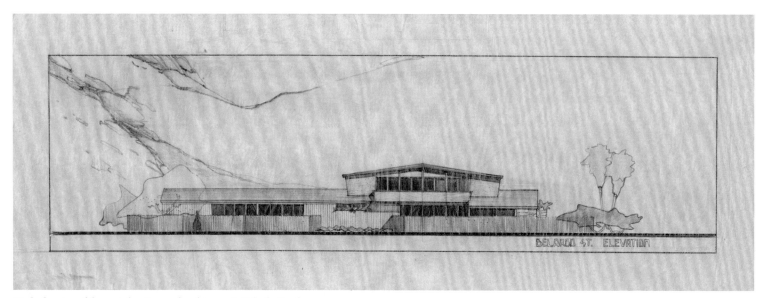

Cody drawing of the east elevation and parking on S. Belardo Road.

The reception area features full-height glass on three sides for views to the pool, breezeway, and street.

Second-floor room overlooking the pool, with furniture by Maurice Martiné.

The unique ground-floor apartment with stone wall and slanted door, now known as the William Cody Corner Room.

# Dorothy Levin Residence

Palm Springs | California | 1947

Even before he started studying at USC, Cody had designed houses for Cliff May, the influential developer responsible for thousands of modest modern homes throughout Southern California. A low, L-shaped house, the Levin Residence continues the themes of simplicity, openness, and indoor-outdoor living that characterized many of the May developments. By this time, the L-plan had become common for modern houses, used for instance by Frank Lloyd Wright in his Usonian houses of the 1930s, and more locally by Albert Frey in the Raymond Loewy Residence in Palm Springs (1946). The siting of the Levin Residence gives privacy on the street side, and the outdoor living area is protected by an adobe wall.

For this house, Cody used a 3-by-5-foot grid in the living areas and the main courtyard, emphasized by redwood strips embedded in the concrete floor. This grid ties together the living room and courtyard, which are separated only by full-height windows and sliding glass doors. Cody's desire to create a variety of spaces within a simple plan can be seen in the glass-roofed solarium of the entry foyer that adjoins the living room and kitchen, and also in the folding wooden doors that allow the den to be converted to a more private bedroom; the kitchen, too, can be partially closed off by shutting the folding doors above the counter. These partitions allow flexibility within the relatively open plan of the house. Emily Laser was the decorator for the house, and Eckbo, Royston & Williams the landscape architects. This Los Angeles firm soon became one of most renowned modernist landscape firms in California.

Although a modest house in scale and materials, the Levin Residence was published in *Architectural Record* (February 1950) and in volume 4 of the Japanese series *World's Contemporary Architecture* (1953); in the latter, which was a volume on contemporary American houses, the Levin Residence appeared alongside works such as the Eames House, Philip Johnson's Glass House, and Frank Lloyd Wright's Fallingwater.

View from the entrance solarium through the living room to the patio.

View from the southwest showing the Palm Springs landscape at the beginning of postwar development.

The patio and west side of the living room.

The solarium seen through the kitchen pass-through window.

The hinged wood panels between the kitchen and dining area stack flat against each other when opened. When closed, they abut a matching wood door, creating a continuous floor-to-ceiling surface.

Accordion wood-panel doors create a private space within the open plan.

The corner junction of the living room and the bedroom wing.

The living room with entrance solarium and opaque glass entry doors beyond.

# Haines Studio and Offices

Beverly Hills | California | 1949

Before becoming one of Los Angeles's most famous designers, William Haines was one of Hollywood's most famous actors—according to one survey, the most bankable of all movie actors in 1930. However, he left the industry in 1934 and opened William Haines Designs with partner Jimmie Shields. The firm prospered through commissions for Hollywood friends such as Joan Crawford, Carole Lombard, and George Cukor. Closely identified with the development of Hollywood Regency interiors and one of the pivotal design offices in Southern California, the firm continued to thrive until Haines's retirement in the early 1970s.

Completed in 1949, the Haines Studio and Offices housed rental spaces in the front of the lot and the Haines Studio in the back. The front of the building is set at a slight angle to the street, creating a dynamic composition that draws visitors toward the studio's entry courtyard on the left side of the site. Although Haines's own designs were, not surprisingly, far more theatrical, Cody's plan shows a clean, elegant composition of horizontal and vertical planes in brick, glass, and copper. For instance, a band of copper spans from one side of the site to the other, covering the low wall of the second-floor deck and serving as a unifying visual element. In spite of its modest scale, the Haines Studio and Offices is a rich and subtle

three-dimensional design. In the Haines Studio area, the simplicity of the spaces allowed the architecture to recede to the background and become a stage for Haines's work. Full-height windows on the north provided the consistent light crucial to best showing the colors of Haines's designs.

The Haines Studio also received notice in volume 2 of *World's Contemporary Architecture* alongside such iconic works as the Museum of Modern Art in New York, the United Nations Headquarters, and the Philadelphia Savings Fund Society building.

View from the northwest, showing Cody's abstract composition of plaster, copper, and brick planes.

From the courtyard, the door is set in concentric frames of recessed brick, where its overall geometric pattern contrasts to its white horizontal handle.

Haines Studio entry foyer with north garden courtyard visible through full-height window.

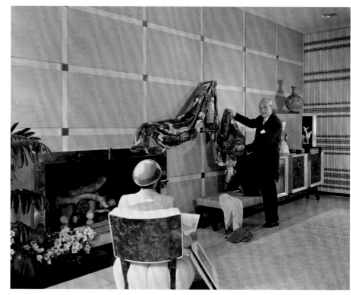

William Haines with a client. The wall is composed of bleached cork panels and bleached ash rails and stiles, with brass squares matching the fireplace surround. The planter at left is black marble.

Although the copper wall of the second-floor balcony parallels the property line, the body of the building is set at an angle.

Newel post detail showing how the steel tube passes through the steel, square-section handrail and concrete tread.

Detail of the north wall, showing the angled section with horizontal openings. The black gate is not original.

# Thunderbird Country Club Clubhouse and Master Plan

Rancho Mirage  |  California  |  1950

Cody's work at Thunderbird Country Club proved pivotal not only to his own career, but also to the development of the Coachella Valley into "the winter golf capital of the world," as local boosters proudly claim. Until 1946, when the Thunderbird Dude Ranch was established, most of the land on which the country club now stands was undeveloped desert. In 1949, the developer and amateur golfer Johnny Dawson teamed with Barney Hinkle to purchase the 663 acres of the ranch—which had not proved profitable—and turn it into a new country club. The club's great draw was to be the first eighteen-hole golf course in the area, and Dawson and Hinkle quickly found investors, including Bob Hope, Bing Crosby, and Desi Arnaz and Lucille Ball. Lawrence Hughes was hired to design the golf course, and Cody was enlisted to construct new buildings and adapt the existing ranch structures for country club use, for instance by adding a new cocktail bar and locker rooms. This was the origin of a successful and influential team: Cody would later work with Dawson and Hughes on several other projects, including Mission Valley Country Club in San Diego and Eldorado Country Club in Indian Wells.

At its opening in 1951, Thunderbird Country Club boasted several major innovations. It is said to have been the first country club to sell residential lots along its fairways—an idea proposed by Cody—establishing

with Thunderbird Country Club Estates a model soon copied all over the country. In addition, Cody is credited with ensuring that no walls were erected on the residential lots within a prescribed distance from the fairways, a condition enforced by deed restrictions. This ensured that the golf course and the homes would form a unified, harmonious landscape. Thunderbird is also notable for being the first club to use motorized golf carts, which were invented by a club member and introduced in 1951.

Thunderbird was an immediate success, and in 1955 it became the first California course to host the biennial Ryder Cup; four years later, another project involving Cody, Dawson, and Hughes—Eldorado Country Club—would become the second. Thunderbird attracted members from all over the nation, including many influential executives. It may even have been the source of the name for Ford's iconic Thunderbird convertible—Ernest R. Breech, chairman of Ford Motor Company, was a Thunderbird member and is said to have asked the club for permission to use it.

Cody's work for Thunderbird included a residential master plan, a new clubhouse, service buildings, and fourteen cottages. The Thunderbird Dude Ranch had been designed by Gordon Kaufmann, a prominent Southern California architect, to resemble the low,

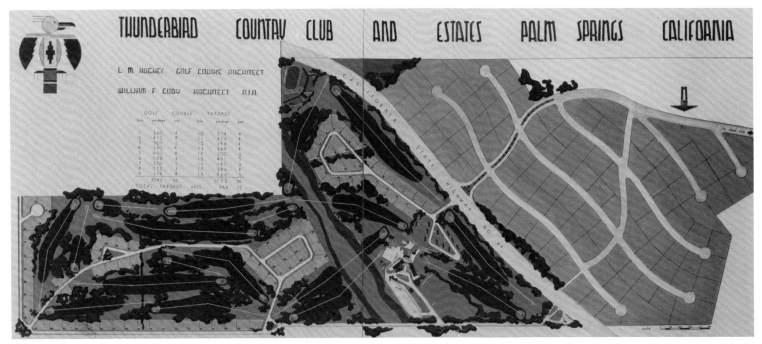

Thunderbird Country Club and Estates master plan by William Cody and golf course architect Lawrence Hughes.

informal, wooden buildings of historical California ranches, albeit with larger windows for better light and views. In 1953, Cody completed major work on the clubhouse building, expanding the kitchen and dining areas and adding a U-shaped wing with locker rooms and pro shop. Of particular importance was the bar, lounge, and dining area with tiered seating allowing uninterrupted views to the first tee.

In addition to work on the country club buildings, Cody designed Thunderbird Estates homes for many club members, including Dawson, Hinkle, and the Texas oilman D.B. McDaniel, whose $100,000 investment had completed Dawson and Hinkle's deal for the dude ranch land. In 1959, Cody designed the plan for the gated community of Thunderbird Heights Estates, just southwest of the country club.

Club president Johnny Dawson and William Cody.

Cody's clubhouse remodel drawing for the north terrace at Tee One, c. 1949.

Cottages are bordered by landscaping, golf paths, and seasonal flowers.

Thunderbird Country Club Team. Left to right: architect William F. Cody, project investor William Jason, founder Frank Bogert, golf course architect Lawrence Hughes, golf club developer and founder Johnny Dawson, realtor Barney Hinkle, project investor Paul Browne and Coachella Valley publicist Anthony Burke.

The step-down bar and continuous windows allow unobstructed views toward the first tee.

Postcard showing putting green next to the clubhouse.

# William F. and Wini Cody Residence

Palm Springs │ California │ 1952

When Cody began designing a home for his family in 1946, he joined a remarkable group of architects developing steel-framed residences in the service of new visions of postwar building and living. Contemporaneous examples include Richard Neutra's 1947 Kaufmann House in Palm Springs, Philip Johnson's 1949 Glass House in New Canaan, Connecticut, and Mies van der Rohe's 1951 Farnsworth House in Plano, Illinois. *Arts & Architecture* magazine's Case Study House Program publicized other innovative solutions, including the 1949 Eames House in Pacific Palisades, California. Within this exceptional set of houses, the Cody Residence reveals distinctive approaches to materials, spaces, and living patterns.

The house's six-year gestation derived from several factors, including postwar steel shortages and Cody's perfectionism. Ultimately, Joseph Malone, for whom Cody had designed a house across the street, helped expedite delivery of the steel from Paramount Steel Company in Long Beach and construction began in October 1948. The framing comprises 3-inch-square columns and a roof measuring only 4 inches in depth, creating an unusually light and unobtrusive structure. Steel offered more than just a modern aesthetic: *The Desert Sun* quoted Wini, mother of three girls, as saying, "daughter control was designed into the home when Bill designed to use steel." Namely, steel allowed large glass areas and undivided interiors that let her keep an eye on Diane, Lynne, and Cathy. This sense of spaciousness is furthered by sixteen floor-to-ceiling sliding glass doors that allow easy access to the exterior from all major spaces.

Unlike many other steel-framed houses, though, the Cody Residence showcases a broad range of materials and textures. For instance, corrugated aluminum covers outdoor spaces such as the carport and breezeways and most of the exterior walls are sheathed in vertical wood siding; a few areas are covered in tile. An adobe wall surrounds much of the building, its roughness complementing the boulders, saguaros, barrel cacti, and other desert plants of Cody's landscape design. It even zigs in places to avoid disturbing several native creosote bushes. Overall, although a strikingly modernist structure, the Cody Residence settles convincingly into its site, with broad, shallow steps that accommodate elevation changes and help define outdoor spaces. Some of these steps extend through the interior, creating several different levels in this one-story structure.

Its layout and massing also distinguish the Cody Residence from many other steel houses of the era. In contrast with the simple, rectangular volumes of

View of the living room from the northeast, showing conversation pit and game table at far left and folding panel doors to the primary bedroom at right. Painting on the wall is by landscape artist and cartoonist James Swinnerton, a longtime family friend.

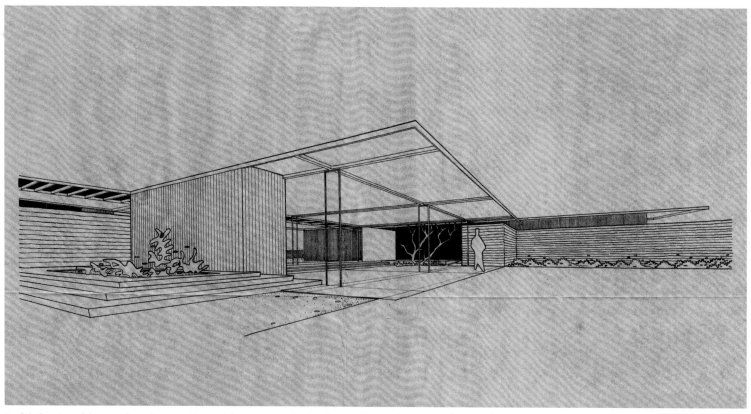

Cody's drawing of the view from the street showing the exceptionally thin planes of the roofs, including (from left) the turquoise-glass awning over the entry passage, the carport canopy, and the kitchen roof.

the Eames House or Farnsworth House, for instance, Cody planned a complex arrangement that relates interior rooms to exterior spaces. The living room, for example, opens to a patio to the west, a garden to the east, and to an open atrium to the north. A retractable canvas awning secures shade for the patio, which is paved with the same tile as the living room floor. The two detached guest rooms form separate wings, each connected to the main house by a breezeway. All of the major rooms have views of nature, often both of gardens adjacent to the house and mountains in the distance.

Water features play multiple roles at the Cody Residence. During the day, they contrast with the landscape, offering relief from the heat and brilliance of the desert. After dark, they create dramatic effects: illuminated from below, the rectangular pools outside the dining area and the master bedroom cast dancing patterns on the walls, while the square pool outside the front guest room centers on a flickering gas flame.

Like the exterior, the interior displays a variety of materials and finishes. Exposed steel columns and beams support a ceiling of clear-coated, tongue-in-groove Douglas fir boards; between the dining area and kitchen these boards were originally painted deep red to mark the spatial transition. Although many walls are composed of sliding glass doors, vertical 1-inch by 6-inch oak paneling lines one wall in the living room and one in the master bedroom. The living room's sunken conversation pit is floored with flagstones.

Throughout the interior, Cody introduced custom features that show off architectural ingenuity, modern technology, and desert living. For instance, the master bedroom suite boasts an exterior garden shower and both guest room showers open to small, private gardens. Instead of standard interior doors, Cody used a floor-to-ceiling, three-panel accordion door between living room and master bedroom, a center-pivot door between living room and children's room, and a concealed paneled door between master bedroom and bomb shelter (also used as a vault). High-tech devices of the day include radiant floor heating, a chiller system for refrigeration, and an intercom connecting doorbell, kitchen, master bedroom, and front guest house. Above the master bed, an electrically operated ceiling panel slides open for evening stargazing.

If Cody designed this home in part to display architectural innovation and technological advances,

Cody's drawing of the front guesthouse interior with its entry court at left and square pool with unexecuted brazier at right. The broad stairs continue to the exterior, the upper tread forming a pocket planter.

he also conceived it as a family project. Throughout the long construction period, whenever he worked on the house he took his wife Wini and his elder daughters Diane and Lynne (Cathy was yet to be born), making the site a home away from home. He even installed a low, wall-hung drinking fountain outside for the girls. With six years spent on design and construction, his family home was the longest project of Cody's career, and many of the techniques and elements he developed for it reappeared throughout his career. Floor-to-ceiling glazing, water features, the integration of internal and external spaces, the juxtaposition of diverse materials, and close attention to detail would continue to characterize his residential designs. As one sign of this building's originality and importance, *Arts & Architecture*, the primary professional journal of modernist architecture, featured it in September 1952. Fortunately, it still stands today, albeit in somewhat modified condition.

Seen from the adobe-walled entry court of the front guesthouse, the entry awning of turquoise glass shades the laid tile entry which continues into the house.

View of the street facade with entry canopy over exterior door at center and storage closet at right. Partially hidden by the foreground adobe wall are the front guest room and its courtyard.

The patios are floored with the same tile as the primary bedroom at left and living room beyond. The black concrete steps in the background continue through the house, dividing the living room from the dining and entry areas.

Cody's drawing of the living room toward the atrium and bedrooms, emphasizing the transparency of the house. The triangular, copper-hooded fireplace was not executed.

Lynne and Diane beneath the steel framing for the front guesthouse, circa 1952.

The vertical wood siding, paired T-section steel supports, translucent-glass screen wall, and corrugated aluminum roofing creates contrasting linear patterns in the carport.

Bill and his daughters (from left) Lynne, Cathy, and Diane in the entry, with the turquoise-colored safety-glass awning visible outside behind them.

Bill and Diane on site next to the adobe blocks used for exterior walls such as the one seen in the background, circa 1946.

# L'Horizon Hotel

Palm Springs | California | 1952

Completed in 1952 for businessman and TV producer Jack Wrather and his wife, film actress and producer Bonita Granville, L'Horizon Hotel presents another novel approach to desert leisure and living. Cody designed a house for the Wrathers on the northeast corner of the site and planned for ten vacation cottages on the rest of the property (only seven were constructed); as built, each of the cottages contains three units. The swimming pool serves as the core of the complex, and grassy lawns cover most of the remaining land. The Wrathers conceived L'Horizon not as just another hotel, but as a place for their Hollywood friends to relax in the desert. Overall, L'Horizon feels more like an intimate neighborhood than a conventional resort or hotel—an atmosphere bolstered by its exclusive clientele.

Cody designed the cottages as Y-shaped buildings, each rotated to a different angle to create variety and preserve privacy; the shifting axes ensure that rooms do not directly face those in other buildings. Each unit has a small terrace, and the bathroom showers face small enclosed gardens. Adobe walls, the simple wood structure, and full-height windows create the setting for casual but sophisticated living.

By the early 2000s, after half a century of weathering, the buildings of L'Horizon had suffered significant deterioration, and the complex was demolished in order to rebuild according to the original drawings. The reconstructed hotel was completed in 2007 and relaunched in 2015 as L'Horizon Resort and Spa, a more luxurious resort. Fortunately, the extensive renovations did not fundamentally change Cody's planning or building exteriors.

Reception office.

Aerial view from west, with Wrather residence at lower left.

Corner of a cottage showing the adobe brick wall that encloses the patio.

Open spaces and the orientation of the cottages provide views and privacy for the occupants.

The rear white painted slump block wall of the apartment angles outward, widening the view of the landscaping and poolside.

# H. Austin Peterson-Frank Sinatra Residence

Rancho Mirage | California | 1953

Frank Sinatra had previously built a home in Palm Springs designed by E. Stewart Williams, a commission that jump-started Williams's career as a modernist. However, Sinatra stayed there for only five years, selling it in 1953. Many of Sinatra's friends were acquiring second homes near the newly completed Tamarisk Country Club in Rancho Mirage, where Cody had designed the clubhouse in 1952, in association with Martin Stern Jr. Cody also created a home for H. Austin Peterson on the seventeenth fairway, which Peterson showed to his friend Sinatra soon after completion. Impressed with the house and the country club, Sinatra made Peterson an offer, becoming the first inhabitant of the house and a member of Tamarisk in March 1954. In its rough stone walls and exposed wood structure, the Peterson Residence recalls the Del Marcos Apartment Hotel, while its pinwheel plan shows similarities with the cottages of L'Horizon Hotel.

Cody's concept for the Peterson Residence was modest: two bedrooms and a guest room in addition to the usual living spaces; the construction permit issued in April 1953 gave a building cost of only $14,134. In 1954, Sinatra's career was at a temporary low, but as his career revived, he commissioned an additional bedroom and bathroom from Cody in 1956. He later purchased more land adjacent to his original plots and, in the ensuing years, constructed cottages, an unpermitted heliport, a lighted tennis court, and many other additions—none by Cody. Sinatra lived in the compound until selling it 1995 because of declining health.

Postcard of Frank Sinatra home.

Cody landscaped the lot with large boulders, integrating the building into the landscape. Sinatra's bedroom is on the left; the designer of the octagonal guesthouse is unknown.

# Mission Valley Country Club and Hotel

San Diego | California | 1954

Too often categorized as a desert modernist, Cody in fact worked extensively outside the Coachella Valley, as far afield as Cuba and Mexico. In San Diego, prior to the Mission Valley Country Club and Hotel commission, Cody had designed the Lippitt Car Wash and had teamed with Paul R. Williams to design the La Jollan Hotel, which opened in 1953. The country club project, though, offered a scale and visibility that helped confirm Cody as a major architect outside the Palm Springs area.

Mission Valley Country Club was the brainchild of the golf course architect Lawrence Hughes, who acquired 225 acres of land to build a new course north of downtown San Diego. Along with Johnny Dawson, Hughes created a semiprivate club with a twenty-seven-hole course. In 1952, he decided to transform the club into a more elaborate, private club, hiring Cody—with whom he had worked at Thunderbird Country Club in Rancho Mirage—to design a new clubhouse complex. Cody brought Maurice Martiné into the project for furniture and interiors.

For the clubhouse, completed in 1954, Cody generated a dynamic composition to exploit angles, views, and outdoor spaces. Seen from the approach, the complex at first would appear solid and imposing,

with a rectangular volume hovering over the entry colonnade. Entering this colonnade of angled, oblong pillars, visitors would first encounter a triangular building housing the lobby and offices. Once past the offices, though, the compound would open up to sun and space on both sides. To the west he set up the pool, locker rooms, and terrace, with nine hotel rooms atop the colonnade overlooking the pool; additional rooms were planned for future construction. To the east of the colonnade would be the major dining areas: the dining patio with reflecting pool, the main dining room, the glass-enclosed garden room, and the sunken bar. The latter two spaces, offset three steps down from the main level, would command outstanding views over the golf course.

Throughout the completed complex, Cody juxtaposed various shapes and materials to strong effect. For example, the clean, rectangular form of the hotel rooms were seen against the playful, irregular shape of the pool, while the simple rectangle of the dining room contrasted with the sawtooth-shaped garden room and the angular sunken bar. Cody exposed the steel structural columns in some places, for instance along the glass walls of the dining room, but concealed them behind plaster in others, notably in the sculptural supports of the entry colonnade.

Nine hotel rooms above the entry colonnade overlook the pool and terrace.

The columns of the colonnade are painted chocolate brown over a built-up plaster form that surrounds a four-inch steel column. Note the contrasting paving of smooth concrete and stone aggregate.

After receiving the Mission Valley commission in 1952, Cody opened a San Diego office on Rosecrans Street, keeping it until about 1957. Henry Hester, another talented modernist and USC graduate, met Cody in 1954 and became the associate project manager for Cody's San Diego clients. In 1957, Hester moved to Cody's San Francisco office to oversee Cody's project for a large, low-income residential development in Contra Costa County; when this project fell through, he returned to San Diego and continued his career as one of the area's finest modernist architects.

Mission Valley Country Club was renamed Stardust Country Club in 1962, and the golf course was completely redesigned in the 1990s when the San Diego Trolley line was extended through the area. In spite of changes of ownership and subsequent modifications, though, the basic outlines of Cody's concept, especially the distinctively shaped swimming pool, remain visible in parts of the Handlery Hotel now occupying the site.

View from entry colonnade to pool patio, with locker rooms in the background on the right.

Shallow steps lead to the entry colonnade beneath the cantilevered building.

View from bar to the lounge, which is enclosed by glass on both sides.

The semioval columns of the entry colonnade are set at an oblique angle. The pool terrace and locker rooms are visible through the sliding glass doors.

Opening celebration, January 19, 1955. From left to right, Wini and Bill Cody, Mrs. and Carl Mueller, Lawrence and Mrs. Hughes, and actress Dolores Michaels with her husband, designer Maurice Martiné.

Seen from the east, the pool shows Cody's flair for dynamic, custom shapes.

An exterior stairway with angled supports and custom steelwork.

# Earle E. Jorgensen Residence

Rancho Mirage | California | 1955

One of many houses that Cody designed in Thunderbird Country Club Estates, the Jorgensen Residence shows how his home designs had evolved since the smaller houses of the 1940s, such as the Levin Residence. Built on an irregularly shaped lot, the Jorgensen Residence is composed of different wings that reach out to embrace exterior spaces, including a pool, a grass court, and a motor court. This kind of asymmetrical pinwheel plan was an archetypal modern invention, seen for instance in Palm Springs at the Kaufmann Desert House by Richard Neutra. Cody employed this kind of plan to relate each major interior space to an exterior garden or terrace, creating a great range of environments to support informal entertaining. For instance, a deep roof overhang covers the patio outside the living room, establishing a shaded area that links the interior with the pool. Each of the bedrooms enjoys views, as well as showers that open onto private patios from which occupants can access the pool.

As usual, Cody's carefully designed details contribute to the clarity of the architecture. For example, the huge sheet of glass in the entry is set directly into the floor, walls, and ceiling, ensuring that no moldings or frames distract from the view. Similarly, the wooden blinds in the living room disappear into a recess above the ceiling plane when raised. Terrazzo floors carry through from the interior to the patios, further eliminating barriers between inside and outside.

In this luxurious house, Cody was able to employ a wide range of expressive materials. Sixty-five tons of fieldstone form the masonry walls and fireplace, and the bathroom counters are made of Roman travertine. Most of the interior walls are lined with wormy chestnut or black walnut. For instance, folding doors in wormy chestnut conceal the bar and music alcove, the tableware and linen closets, and the door to the kitchen, creating a continuous expanse of wall when closed.

Remarkably, the work of the interior designer Helen Conway remains visible throughout the house. In 1957, only two years after its completion, the Jorgensens sold it to Paul A. and Katharine O. Mavis. Always used as a vacation home, the house has not experienced the wear and tear of a primary residence. Over the years, Katharine Mavis preserved the original architecture and interiors, even ordering custom fabrics to replace worn originals. Still owned by the Mavis family, today this house offers the closest approach to a time capsule of any of Cody's works.

Shallow steps frame the north and east sides of the swimming pool.

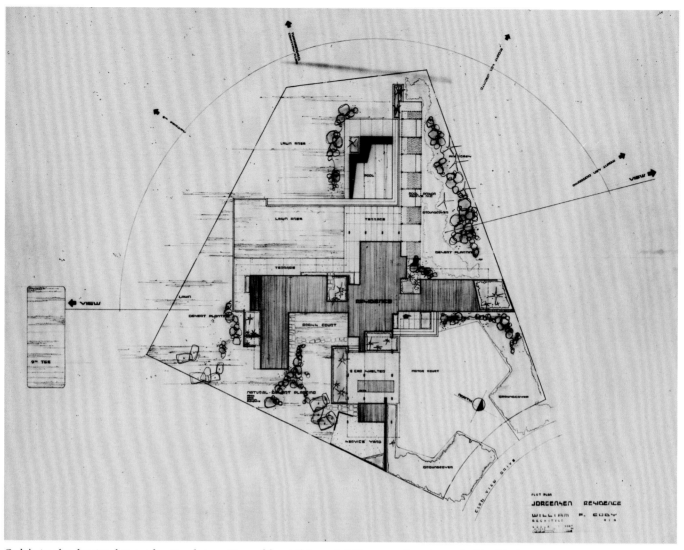

Cody's site plan drawing showing directional views. Views of the ninth tee and clubhouse are from the south side of the house.

Design rendering by Cody.

The floor-to-ceiling entry doors, common in Cody's houses, open to views of a garden across the foyer.

A wall of knotted wood panel extends from the foyer down the hallway toward the primary bedroom.

The raised hearth is integrated with the ashlar fireplace and wall. In order to minimize visual obstructions between inside and outside, drapes and sunshades hang from recessed tracks in the ceiling.

The glass of the foyer's window wall disappears into the surrounding surfaces, allowing the planes of the room to continue uninterrupted to the outside.

A deep roof overhang shades the terrace and the living room windows. The property wall at right boasts a geometric pattern.

# Villa Real Golfotel

Havana | Cuba | 1955 (unbuilt)

María Teresa (Nena) and Alvaro González Gordon, a prominent Havana couple, contacted Cody to design the Villa Real Golfotel, comprising the Villa Real Country Club, a fifty-room hotel, and a master plan for the site at Colinas de Villareal in Havana. The Gordons may have become familiar with Cody's work from seeing the Del Marcos Apartment Hotel showcased at the 1950 Pan American Exhibition in Cuba.

The design for the Golfotel relies on a variety of angles, a strategy that Cody used in a number of other 1950s projects, including The Springs restaurant and L'Horizon Hotel. His plan sites the Golfotel atop a hill, its wings stretching down the verdant slopes; rectangular cottages are scattered downslope, each facing the views. This was to have been an architecture of conspicuous luxury for Cuban elites.

Cody brought in Maurice Martiné for the interiors and enlisted local architect Raul Portela to manage the project. By October 1956, construction documents had been completed, and by February 1957 the golf course was finished. However, the clients delayed construction on the buildings, and only one bungalow and a bar were in place by the time of a March 30 golf tournament. After that, no more buildings would be constructed, as political conditions forced the

Gordons to abandon the project. However, while working on the Villa Real Golfotel, Cody received four other major country club commissions: Marin Golf & Country Club, Eldorado Country Club, Palo Alto Hills Golf & Country Club, and Round Hill Country Club. He had become perhaps the most sought-after country club architect in California.

After the Cuban Revolution, golf quickly fell from favor as a sport so strongly associated with the capitalism. However, the Villa Real course would be the site of a famous round played by Fidel Castro and Ernesto "Che" Guevara in 1961, undoubtedly intended as a mockery of U.S. capitalism and society. Soon afterward, Castro turned the golf course into a military camp.

The site model shows the clubhouse perched on top of the hill, with other proposed buildings placed parallel to the slope for better views and ease of construction.

Pages 80 – 81: This presentation drawing by Gene Shrewsbury
shows the angular clubhouse within the lush landscape
of Havana, with the Straits of Florida in the background.

# The Springs

Palm Springs | California | 1956

The Springs restaurant was the first building in the Cameron Center, a major project that Cody took on for the real estate developer George Cameron, Jr. Cameron had previously hired Cody to design his own house at Thunderbird Country Club in Rancho Mirage, as well as to work on other projects.

For The Springs—advertised as a restaurant, coffee shop, and cocktail bar—Cameron gave Cody free rein. The result was a building that combined Cody's usual elegance with the expressiveness of commercial architecture. In Southern California at the time, architects such as Armet & Davis were using bright colors, synthetic materials, and neon signs to make restaurants, gas stations, and other common commercial buildings stand out in their urban environments—what later became known as Googie architecture. For Palm Springs, which remained low and uncrowded—in 1956, the population had just passed 10,000—Cody took an alternative approach: he eschewed eye-catching colors and strong vertical elements, instead creating a horizontal building of wood, stone, and glass whose colors complemented the hues of the desert and stood out against the clear blue sky. The one-story building seemed to stretch out toward the desert, with exposed beams, some carrying lightweight shades, pointing at the horizon like javelins.

Although extroverted and arresting in form, The Springs fit beautifully in its environment.

Throughout the design, Cody used a variety of angles to accommodate the irregular corner site, create a dynamic exterior, and produce a set of distinctive interior spaces. Each section of the restaurant boasted a distinct atmosphere. For example, the outdoor patio was bright and casual, with movable canvas sunshades; in contrast, the banquet room was enclosed and intimate. The brightly lit coffee shop area used innovative cantilevered seats that freed the floor from clutter and eased cleaning. Seating areas by the windows were protected by exterior screens that reduced the harshness of the sun without cutting off views.

Working with the interior designer Maurice Martiné and the artist Millard Sheets, Cody produced an entirely custom interior. As Cody's project manager Russell Wade put it, "The only thing in here you can buy (off the shelf) are the nails, screws, and light bulbs." The Springs opened in 1956, and print advertisements capitalized on the unique design, proclaiming, "Palm Springs'—and the world's—most exotic new restaurant: THE SPRINGS in Cameron Center."

A triangular roof section slopes down and separates the parking from the entry.

The roof, rafters, and inlaid entrance doors feature the angles that Cody used throughout the restaurant design.

Cody designed the adjacent Cameron Center to include a hotel, a professional office building, large chain stores, a new car agency, and independent retailers. Ultimately, the project was scaled down, with two large stores—Mayfair Market and Woolworth's—plus smaller shops and offices. Cody opened his office annex in the Woolworth's building, a five-minute walk from his headquarters. The Cameron Center was completed in 1958 but, along with The Springs, has been demolished.

The canvas awnings offer shelter from the desert sun.

The west side of the restaurant, showing the rafter tails that pierce the striped awnings.

Opening of The Springs, December 21, 1956. Standing (L to R), actor and realtor Russell Wade, actor Desi Arnaz, Bill Cody, Springs manager Alan Dale. Seated (L to R), Cameron Center owners Daphne and George Cameron Jr., actress Alice Faye and husband, comedian Phil Harris.

CAMERON CENTER RESTAURANT
WILLIAM F. CODY
ARCHITECT A.I.A.

Early design development perspective.

Angles are everywhere on the northeast patio, including the door, door pull, wall paneling, planting beds, and roof overhang.

The breakfast bar of The Springs has arguably the earliest example of cantilevered stool seating.

On the east side of the restaurant, retractable canvas awnings soften the sunlight on the outdoor dining patio.

A triangular inlaid table in the Oak Room reinforces the angles of the architecture. The large boulder seen through the picture window sits under the sloping roof section at the restaurant's entrance.

The canted fieldstone wall at the entrance to the Oak Room carries a laminated wood beam. The mural on the right is by Millard Sheets.

Cody used a great variety of textures and finish materials, as seen here in the triangular fireplace, tiled counter wall, wooden paneling, and stucco ceiling.

Artist Millard Sheets created the wall mosaics of Native American mythical figures. Maurice Martiné collaborated with Cody for the design of the interior furnishings.

# Edificio Mateal

Havana | Cuba | 1956 (unbuilt)

The Gordons commissioned Cody to design a 14-story mixed-use building in Havana. Edificio Mateal was planned to house a small commercial space on the first floor, offices on floors 2–7, duplex apartments on the next five floors, and a large penthouse apartment on the next floor. The top floor would be for mechanical equipment and an office space Cody and Raul Portela planned to use for future collaborations. Beneath the structure would be two levels of underground parking.

Although a strictly geometric and unornamented concrete structure, the proposal for Edificio Mateal incorporated aspects of local Havana architecture. Like the neighboring existing building, Cody's plan incorporated a ground-floor arcade and upper floors that projected out over the sidewalk. Inspired by vernacular Cuban buildings, Cody also designed louvered storm shutters to provide shade, allow ventilation, and also protect against hurricanes. The project was showcased in *Arts & Architecture* in September 1955.

Cody's perspective drawing of Edificio Mateal highlights the abstract, rectilinear composition formed by the alternating precast concrete panels and wooden shutters. The ground-floor arcade continues the rhythm of the traditional building to the left.

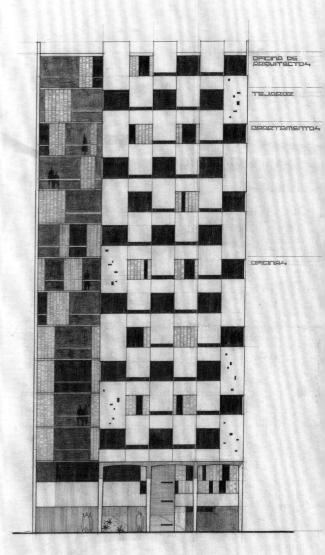

EDIFICIO
MATEAL

WILLIAM F CODY AIA ARQUITECTOS HABANA CUBA
RAUL PORTELA, SOCIO

The ground-floor plan by Cody illustrates parking and a small shop. As shown in the elevation, the top floor was intended as an office for Cody and Portela.

# Eldorado Golf Club Estates Cottages East and West

Indian Wells | California | 1958, 1961

The famed Eldorado Country Club was conceived to be more than just a venue for dining, golf, and recreation—it was also the focus for a community of hundreds of homes, ranging from relatively modest cottages to expansive, luxurious fairway houses. The first homes were the twenty-nine buildings for Eldorado Golf Club Estates Cottages East that Cody designed just east of the clubhouse, which were completed before the clubhouse. He designed an additional twenty-two cottages, completed in 1961, for Cottages West. Each of these complexes would contain only three types of buildings, but Cody avoided any impression of rote repetition by changing the orientations of the buildings and mirroring the plans. In each of the three unit plans in Cottages West (one bedroom, two baths; two bedrooms, three baths; three bedrooms, four baths), the extra bathroom is off the living room, allowing the living room to be partitioned off and used as an extra guest room.

Both complexes were designed as convenient leisure communities with recreational facilities such as putting greens and swimming areas, the latter boasting distinctive elements such as the boomerang-shaped pool at Cottages East and the elegant arcades of shallow arches and sculptural columns at Cottages West. At the western end of Cottages West, backer Robert P. McCulloch planned a Presidential Bungalow,

President John F. Kennedy visiting General Eisenhower in October 1962, photographed near Eisenhower's cottage at Eldorado.

to be owned by the country club and rented to U.S. presidents and other visiting dignitaries; in addition to President Eisenhower, German chancellor Konrad Adenauer would visit the Eldorado. However, John F. Kennedy's 1960 electoral victory over Richard Nixon caused McCulloch and Eldorado to cancel what they had imagined as the "White House of the West." Both Kennedy and Nixon did end up visiting Eisenhower at Eldorado, though—Kennedy in March 1962 and Nixon in February 1965.

Shallow, elegant arches and sculptural columns form the poolside breezeway between the men's and women's changing rooms at the Eldorado Cottages West recreation area.

Presentation drawing by J.R. Hollingsworth showing Eldorado Golf Club Estates Cottages East from the north.

The recreation area with boomerang-shaped pool serves as the focus for Cottages East.

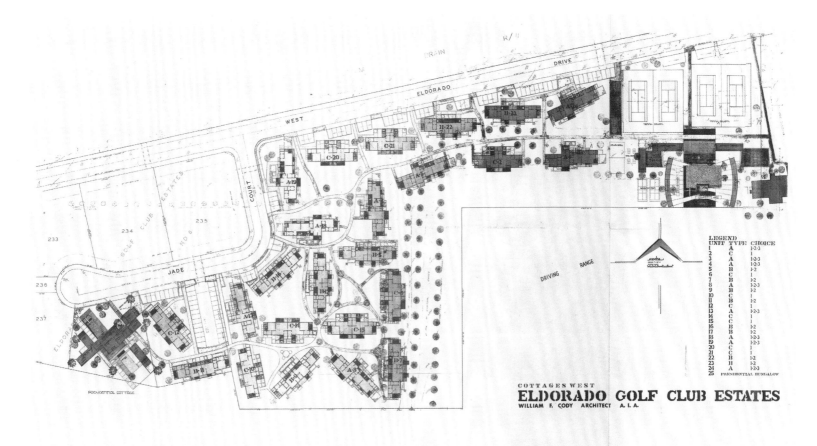

Site plan for twenty-four buildings of Eldorado Golf Club Estates Cottages West, the second Eldorado cottage development. The large residence at the far left is the planned presidential cottage, which included accommodations for the Secret Service and support staff.

The corner post of the overhanging roof together with the concrete-block patio wall form a subtle, abstract composition.

The striated vertical pattern on the exterior wall of this Cottages West unit continues on the planter wall.

The starter building shown here also served as Robert McCulloch's office during clubhouse construction, later becoming the office for Eldorado Properties realtor Russell Wade.

Elevated seating platforms with thin, petal-like roofs and slender steel railings sit at each end of the swimming pool at Cottages West.

The flattened arches of the breezeway are mirrored in the pattern of the aggregate-and-concrete patios.

The elevated poolside platforms provide sheltered spaces slightly distanced from the pool.

# Eldorado Country Club Clubhouse

Indian Wells | California | 1959

Likened to the Taj Mahal and the Palace of Versailles in the promotional material of the day, the Eldorado Country Club clubhouse marks the apex of Cody's designs for exclusive country clubs, displaying the breadth of his design skills as well as a fully mature vision for leisure and living. Funded mainly by the industrialist Robert P. McCulloch, this building showed that an unapologetically modernist structure could serve as an icon for a new model of country club development.

Prior to Eldorado, Cody had established himself as an innovative planner and designer through executed buildings for Thunderbird Country Club, Mission Valley Country Club in San Diego, and Tamarisk Country Club, as well as an unexecuted design for Villa Real Country Club in Havana. At Eldorado, he created the master plan and designed the clubhouses, guest cottages, recreation area, and other secondary buildings. Some of his most remarkable houses—for example the Cannon Residence (1961) and Shamel Residence (1963)—were for Eldorado's private fairway lots.

At Eldorado, Cody worked with interior designer Arthur Elrod and landscape architect John Vogley. The latter was a recent college graduate working in Cody's newly established San Francisco office; Eldorado was Vogley's first major project and helped launch his career. Since the Eldorado project overlapped with other large projects, including the Palm Springs Spa Hotel Bathhouse, the Palo Alto Hills Golf & Country Club, and Round Hill Country Club, Cody relieved the workload on his office by contracting with the office of Ernest J. Kump Associates in Palo Alto to produce construction documents. McCulloch became one of Cody's most important clients, commissioning work in Palm Desert, Rancho Mirage, and Los Angeles, as well as Scottsdale and Lake Havasu in Arizona.

Eldorado gained national renown almost immediately, hosting the 1959 Ryder Cup and welcoming celebrities ranging from Bob Hope to President Eisenhower. The *New York Times* reported in December 1960 that after leaving office Eisenhower would spend two months "in a home on the Eldorado Country Club grounds during a two-month visit here beginning in February." (Dwight and Mamie Eisenhower later commissioned a house from Los Angeles architect Welton Becket for one of the fairway lots, which was completed in 1961.)

The clubhouse, cottages, and various fairway homes show how Cody infused the language of modernism with a sense of place and occasion, complementing austere forms with luxurious details and exquisite

Visitors approach along two walkways flanking a mosaic-tiled pool, entering the clubhouse through two pairs of automatic full-height doors.

Eldorado Country Club clubhouse at sunset.

views. Seen from the south, the pure white portico of the dining terrace rises above the lawn like a temple of leisure. In fact, the *New York Times* noted that Eldorado "resembles a modern palace rather than the homey country clubs of the East." Roger Bullard, a New York architect and clubhouse designer, argued, "I would hold as most important that the architectural design be of such a character that the club house building becomes actually a part of the landscape. Being a type of building modern in its origin, as in its purpose, it is much more important that its design reflect characteristics of this day than that an attempt be made to associate it with any architectural style of the past." Few clients and architects were willing to pursue this principle as thoroughly as McCullough and Cody, though.

Inside the clubhouse, Cody fashioned warmer and more playful spaces, introducing teak, brick, and stone to complement the glass and concrete. With its sweeping views of the golf course and the Santa Rosa Mountains, the dining room served as Eldorado's core. In order to maintain the openness of the interior, in several places Cody used perforated

partitions rather than solid walls. He set off the bar by suspending a gently curved wooden canopy and a small constellation of pendant lamps, all of which he designed himself. Elrod's furniture and furnishings also were planned to work with the architecture to create distinct areas within the expansive dining areas.

Ultimately, Cody's designs and the Eldorado Country Club as a whole served as catalysts for the development of the immediate area into an exclusive enclave. Built on land formerly used as a citrus, date, and grape ranch, Indian Wells became one of the wealthiest cities in the nation after being incorporated in 1967, serving as home to retired executives, Hollywood celebrities, and other affluent individuals. "But even with this group," noted the *New York Times* in 1972, "there is an inner ring of exclusivity and privilege—the 500 members of the El Dorado Country Club." Through realtor Russell Wade and the Eldorado Properties office, which was located on the country club property, Cody met and designed homes for many of these Eldorado elites.

In the evening, the lighting of the fountains and clubhouse enhances the drama of the architecture and setting.

Presentation drawing by J.R. Hollingsworth showing the clubhouse from the south.

From left to right: building contractor Mike Eversz, William Cody, and club president Robert P. McCulloch.

The dining room and terrace float above the pond and cart storage below and offer outstanding views of the fairway and the Santa Rosa Mountains.

View from foyer toward dining room, showing use of open screen walls.

The suspended teak canopy defines the bar area and showcases Cody's pendant lamp designs.

Women's locker room with paneled lockers and custom pendant lamps.

Men's locker room.

Custom door to men's locker room with Cody's type design in bronze..

Mosaic depicting the mythical god of gold, Eldorado, on the wall of the men's locker room sun court.

# Palm Springs Spa

Palm Springs | California | 1959

The Agua Caliente Band of Cahuilla Indians had occupied parts of the Coachella Valley for centuries or even millennia, but the arrival first of the Spanish and then, after California statehood, large numbers of Anglo settlers fundamentally uprooted their culture and livelihoods. In 1876, the federal government created the Agua Caliente Indian Reservation, a patchwork of mostly noncontiguous, 1-mile-square plots in the Coachella Valley and San Jacinto Mountains. One of these plots, Section 14, contained the hot springs that were central to the Agua Caliente culture. This section also happened to be in the middle of Palm Springs, making the Agua Caliente Band the largest corporate landowner in the city.

However, through the 1950s, the band could not develop this reservation land, in part because leases for Indian lands were limited to five years; no developer would commit significant capital without the security of a longer agreement. On August 9, 1955, though, the U.S. Congress approved twenty-five-year leases. On February 13, 1958, developer Samuel W. Banowit signed just such a lease to develop the Agua Caliente Resort Hotel & Spa in Palm Springs, the first long-term commercial lease of Indian lands anywhere in the nation. He stated, "We believe that our project will set the pattern for opening of lands owned by Indian

tribes not only in Palm Springs but in other parts of the West." Agua Caliente Tribal Council chair Vyola J. Ortner, along with local realtors Russell Wade and Lew Levy, introduced Cody to Banowit to design the project. Philip Koenig, a Chicago architect, served as Banowit's representative and project coordinator.

Banowit formed Palm Springs Spa, Inc. to develop the project, planning it in two phases. Phase 1 included the Palm Springs Spa, and phase 2 the Palm Springs Spa Hotel. For the first phase, duties were divided among a team composed of Cody, the firm of Wexler & Harrison, and Koenig. Cody was the design architect, while Wexler & Harrison served as the executive architects and Koenig the project architect. John Vogley of Cody's San Francisco office was the landscape architect, and Maurice Martiné the interior designer.

The defining feature of the spa was a vaulted, concrete arcade that spanned the entire block, serving as a connecting spine for the bathhouse. Although austere in its color and material, its gently curved, precast vaults created an elegant and striking image, especially when seen against the blue of the sky above and the 150-foot-long pool below. Half of the arcade columns in fact stood within the pool, which was lined with

The arcade columns rest on pedestals in the reflecting pool. Los Angeles artist Bernard Zimmerman created the sculpture, which was inspired by Greek water nymphs.

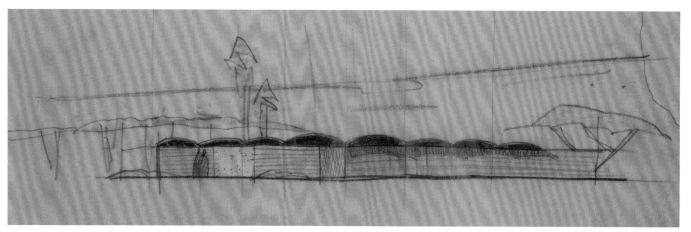

Cody's early sketch showing the forms of the entry arcade vaults.

Italian glass tile in various shades of blue. The entry arcade, as well as the loggia of the outdoor pool area, suggested connections with the great baths of ancient Rome. Cody had drawn shallow-arched arcades as far back as his USC days (see page 288) and used similar motifs throughout his career in projects such as the Nicoletti Residence and unbuilt designs for Tropicana Gardens and Round Hill Country Club (page 259).

Of all Cody's works, the Palm Springs Spa, along with St. Theresa Catholic Church, best embodied his desire to integrate architecture and art. Visitors were greeted by Bernard Zimmerman's metal sculpture at the beginning of the entry arcade and by John Mason's stoneware artworks on the south facade. Once inside, they could view works by Dale Clark as well as Charles and Dextra Frankel.

The bathhouse opened its doors on January 21, 1960, under the name Palm Springs Spa; at the top of the front page, *The Desert Sun* proudly proclaimed, "World's Most Beautiful Spa Opens Today." Only five weeks later, the paper reported that many celebrities had already visited, including boxer Jack Dempsey, dancer Ann Miller, singer Peggy Lee, and Johnny Weissmuller of Tarzan fame. The Palm Springs Spa and the adjoining Spa Hotel (see page 162) were demolished in 2014 in spite of protests from preservationists; the site is now home to the Agua Caliente Cultural Museum, scheduled to open in late 2020.

The roughness and solidity of the fieldstone wall complement the elegance and lightness of the colonnade.

Palm Springs Spa team from left: Russell Wade, William Cody, Lew Levy, and Sam Banowit.

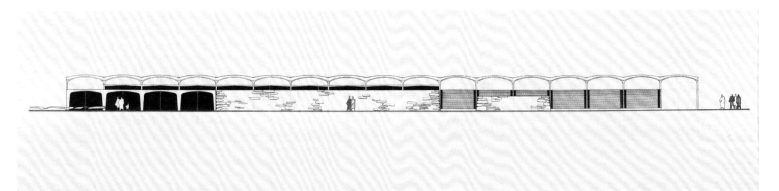

Cody's preliminary design drawing showing the full length of the arcade from the west.

Variations of the shallow arcade arches appear in the paving, bench, and bridge. Los Angeles artist John Mason created the abstract stoneware wall sculptures on the entrance facade.

Rendering of the Palm Springs Spa and Hotel by QA Architectural Arts.

The mineral pool in the foreground is centered around a sculpture by Dextra and Charles Frankel, while the pool beyond is shaded by a scalloped canopy. The third mineral pool is visible in the far background.

The plaque on the freestanding stone wall commemorates the site as "the Mineral Spring which for centuries past has been a shrine and gathering place of the Cahuilla Indians."

The bathhouse entrance lobby looking south, with interior design by Maurice Martiné.

View from the lobby looking north, with the vault of the arcade visible through the lobby ceiling.

View from the lobby looking south, showing the reflecting pool continuing inside and terminating at a drinking fountain supplied by the natural springs.

The sculpture in the men's spa is by California artist Dale Clark.

Earth and stone appear in many guises in the men's changing room: terrazzo floor, river rock wall, planter pebbles, ceiling stucco, and, on the wall at right, decorative tile by artists Dextra and Charles Frankel.

# Racquet Club Cottages West

Palm Springs | California | 1960

One of the most influential developers in Southern California, Paul Trousdale built over 25,000 homes. His most famous project, Trousdale Estates in Beverly Hills, includes houses by many famous modernist architects. In 1957, Johnny Dawson, who had worked with Cody on major country club projects, recommended him to Trousdale to design two California projects: the Marin Golf & Country Club in Novato and the Marin Hotel & Sports Club in San Rafael. Although neither of these designs was executed—apparently because of cost—Trousdale did commission Cody in 1959 to design projects for the Racquet Club in Palm Springs. Actors Charles Farrell and Ralph Bellamy founded the Racquet Club in 1934 as a place where their Hollywood friends could play tennis, and the club remained popular with actors, including stars such as Clark Gable, Kirk Douglas, and Elizabeth Taylor. This clientele helped make it an icon of postwar leisure, a status reinforced by its appearance in national magazine ads for upscale cars such Cadillac's convertibles and Chevrolet's Corvette.

Trousdale asked Cody to create a master plan for a new development that would include cottages, swimming pools, recreation areas, and putting greens. This complex, known as Cottages West, was intended for members of the Racquet Club who found it increasingly difficult to find maids, gardeners, housekeepers, and other staff for their homes. Instead of buying or renting standard homes, they could rent these fully furnished cottages, which came with cleaning, room, and secretarial services. Although Cody's original plan exceeded Trousdale's budget, a modified complex of eighteen cottages with a swimming pool and cabana was completed in 1960.

In order to accommodate a variety of users, Trousdale and Cody developed four types of plans: one-bedroom apartment, living room suite, bedroom suite (no kitchen), and bachelor (no kitchen). By closing a door between the two dressing rooms, the one-bedroom unit can be separated into a living room suite and a bedroom suite. The four unit types were mirrored and combined in various ways to create a wide variety of buildings and exterior spaces, a strategy that Cody had previously used at L'Horizon Hotel. For example, some cottages consist of adjoining two one-bedroom units, while others house only a single one-bedroom or bachelor unit. An artificial creek and curving paths, part of the landscape design by Phil Shipley & Associates, also contribute to the sense of variety and lushness.

Although small in size, the cottages were intended for an elite clientele and boasted Cody's usual

View from east over pool with fountain, with pergola and San Jacinto Mountain in the background.

The interiors are designed for casual living, with protected patios and open views.

refined design. He created simple, elegant planes for roofs and walls, removing distracting elements. For example, he seated the floor-to-ceiling glass directly in the sill, mullions, and header, obviating the need for obtrusive moldings; this was his favored hush-and-flush technique. He avoided crown and base moldings inside, ensuring that the floor, walls, and ceiling met cleanly and clearly. Even when using modest materials, he was able to create appealing effects, as seen for instance in the screen walls of concrete block.

Although the Racquet Club itself no longer exists, Cottages West remains, now known as Racquet Club Garden Villas. In 2013, it was designated a historic district by the Palm Springs City Council.

Rendering of a typical Cottages West unit by J.R. Hollingsworth.

The cottages are modest in size but show a number of Cody's distinctive touches, such as floor-to-ceiling glass and patterned screen walls.

Eastern entrance to the complex with cottage and artificial creek.

J.R. Hollingsworth rendering of Racquet Club Cottages West. The project was ultimately scaled back to left (east) part of the site shown here, including the pool area and about half of the cottages.

# Louise Durham Nicoletti Residence

Rancho Mirage | California | 1961

High in the hills of Thunderbird Ranch Estates, the Nicoletti Residence is sometimes described as "Little Eldorado" because its elevated siting and white porticoes resemble those of Cody's Eldorado Country Club Clubhouse. Designed as an opulent home for entertaining, this house is large in scale—enclosing 4,500 square feet and boasting extensive porches and terraces—but modest in program: it contains a master bedroom and living spaces in the main house, plus detached guest quarters and a detached maid's room. The living room measures 40 feet by 20 feet and features a unique bar that is part inside and part outside; it is divided in half by a floor-to-ceiling sliding glass door. Deep porches create shaded areas to the northeast and southwest of the living room, the former looking toward Thunderbird Country Club and the latter to the pool and nearby mountains.

The dominant motif for the house is a shallow arch, used in the living room and large porticoes, as well as in the entry, pool cabana, and guest room shade structure; it even appears at the top of the iron railing on the elevated terrace and in the shape of the pool. Cody also used the arch beneath the living room terrace for the facade of the basement level, which housed Nicoletti's large workspace, cold storage for furs, and a utility room. Maxine Overbeck was the

A sliding glass door passes through the middle of the indoor/outdoor bar, allowing the interior to be closed off from the porch.

interior decorator, and her designs contrasted strongly with the modernist bent of the architecture. Charles Darland was the landscape designer and William Foster the contractor.

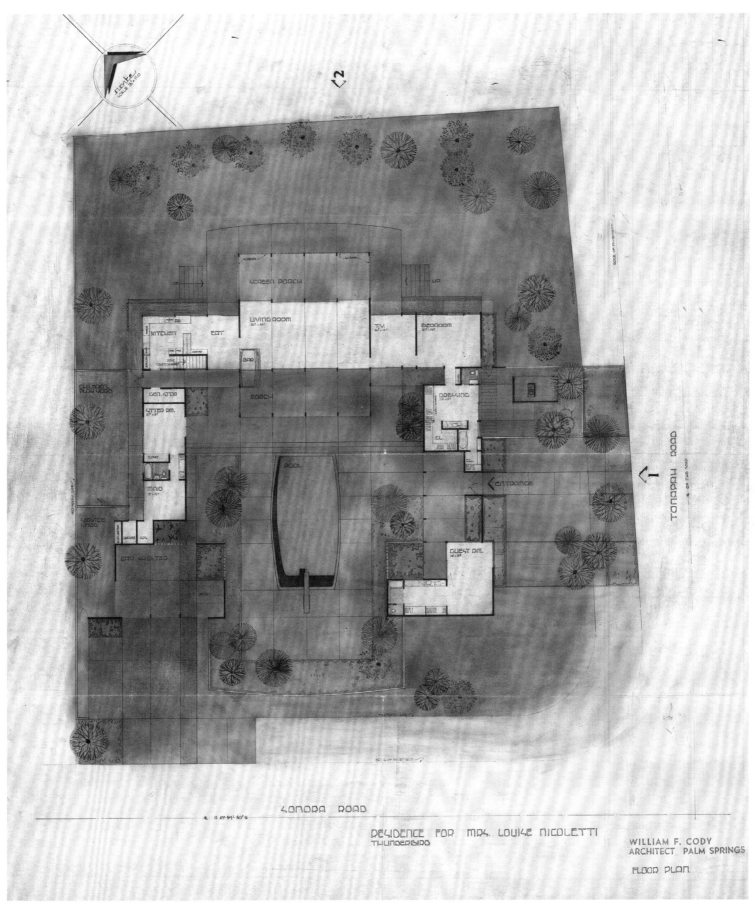

Plan drawing by Cody showing how the house was designed with a large living room and expansive porches for entertaining large groups of guests.

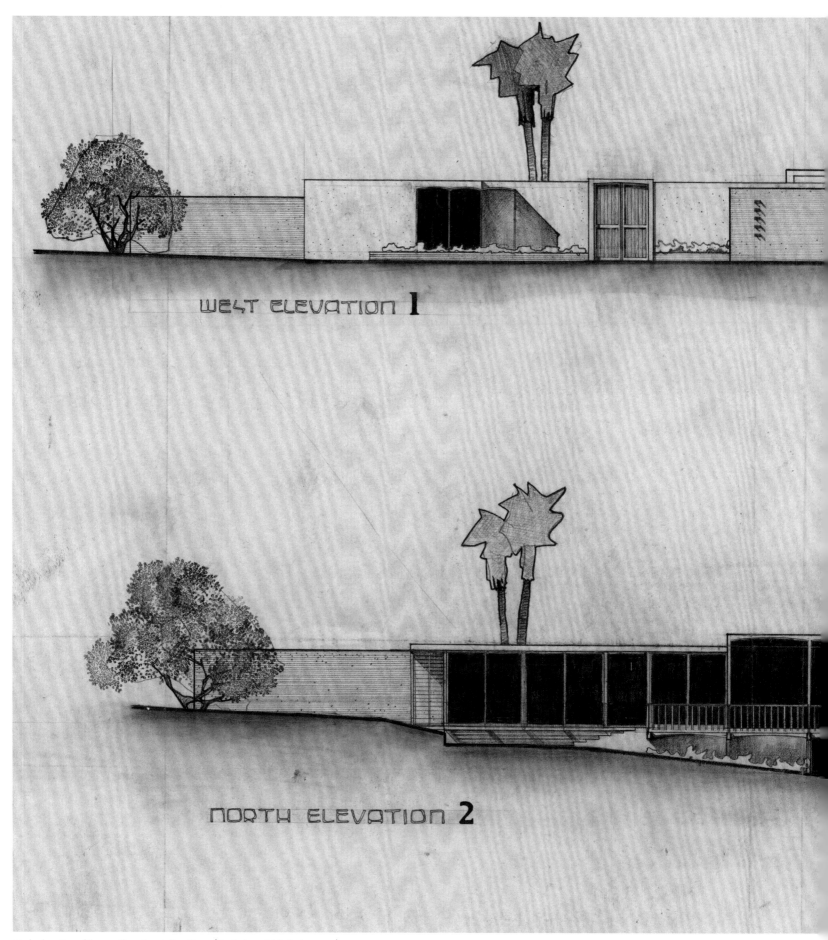

WEST ELEVATION 1

NORTH ELEVATION 2

Cody drawing of the north and east elevations (the latter mislabeled as west).

View from southern shade canopy through the living room to the valley. The sliding glass doors that line the living room open to create an expansive indoor/outdoor entertaining area.

Entry facade showing the guesthouse to the left of the entry and the main house to the right.

Cody under the loggia between the living room and the pool.

The scalloped ceiling extends from the living room to the north terrace and the south pool patio. Seen on the left in the corner of the room is the start of the indoor/outdoor bar.

As in his other residential designs, in the Nicoletti Residence Cody uses paneled cabinet doors to create continuous surfaces of wood.

# Palo Alto Hills
# Golf & Country Club

Palo Alto | California | 1961

The clubhouse for the Palo Alto Hills Golf &
Country Club continued Cody's run of luxurious golf
clubhouses in the late 1950s. At 32,500 square feet,
the Palo Alto building was similar in both scale and
architectural design to the slightly earlier Eldorado
Country Club Clubhouse in Indian Wells. In both
examples, the main section was a clean, rectangular
structure with a deep, columned porch that looked
toward the fairways. An alternate design with sloping
roofs and angular stone walls showed strong affinities
with Cody's designs at the Lemurian Fellowship.

Palo Alto Hills Golf & Country Club opened in 1962,
and expansions and alterations have covered up
Cody's original design. However, the outlines of some
of the major elements—notably the main building and
its porch, as well as the pool—remain visible today.

The fairway side of the clubhouse as delineated by J.R. Hollingsworth.

128

# W. & J. Sloane Company Display House

La Quinta | California | 1961

Founded in New York in 1842, the furniture and design store W. & J. Sloane was known for furnishing elite residences, including the White House and the Breakers, Cornelius Vanderbilt's Newport mansion. The company also operated stores in California, commissioning its Beverly Hills store, completed in 1950, from renowned Los Angeles architect Paul R. Williams. To promote its products, the Sloane Company furnished a number of model homes in Southern California, many designed by prominent architects such as Williams and William Sutherland Beckett. For the Sloane Display House in La Quinta, intended to promote Sloane's Palm Springs studio, Cody was the architect and John Vogley the landscape architect; Guy Roop of Sloane's San Francisco studio was the interior designer.

The Sloane La Quinta house was also supported by Southern California Gas Company (SoCalGas), whose heavily promoted "Balanced Power" model homes used natural gas for not only cooking and heating, but also refrigeration and air-conditioning. Cody's elaborate house was distinctive among these Balanced Power homes, most of which were more typical houses in new residential neighborhoods and planned communities. A model house not only for Sloane and SoCalGas, but also for desert

architecture, the La Quinta residence opened to the public on March 18, 1961. A SoCalGas advertisement exclaimed, "You'd expect a $200,000 home to have the best of everything. This elegant BALANCED POWER home has exactly that!" In fact, the house was a persuasive exhibition of Cody's preferred design strategies, including carefully considered indoor/outdoor relationships, water features, and dynamic floor plans.

With its entry arcade, pool terrace, courtyards, and loggias occupying as much space as the house proper, the Sloane Display House embodied an ideal of indoor/outdoor life in which outdoor spaces are as important as interior rooms. Water was everywhere: ponds greeting visitors in the motor court and by the entry wall and a decorative pool with fountains running between the main house and the guest quarters on the west. The swimming pool functioned as the focus of the leisure spaces, its complex shape echoing the forms of the rest of the house. All of these elements were brought together in a complex plan whose elements seem to flow out into the landscape.

In addition to the floor-to-ceiling glass and steel structural elements that Cody employed so effectively, two interior elements stood out. One was the thin-

Part of an extensive set of water features, this pool extends the entry axis and emphasizes the separation of the main house to the left and the guest room and maid's quarters to the right.

The curved adobe wall to the left of the carport terminates in a rectangular pool with fountain. Cody used circular forms not only in the motor court but also for the bedroom patios.

shell concrete vaulting of the living room, which seemed to float above the walls, separated by a glass clerestory. The other was the custom, three-legged fireplace whose curves complemented those of the ceiling. Cody repeated the gentle curves of the ceiling in the entry arcade roof, whose supports were set on pedestals in the pond, similar to those of the entranceway at the Palm Springs Spa.

The Sloane Display House was recognized in 1962 by the Homes for Better Living Awards program, which was sponsored by the American Institute of Architects in cooperation with *House & Home* and *Life* magazine. The house is extant but has been heavily remodeled.

Cody repeated the gentle curve of the entry canopy in the oblong shapes of the paving and the roof overhang openwork.

The columns of the entry canopy rest on pedestals in the water, a technique that Cody also used for the arcade of the Palm Springs Spa. In both projects, the entry spine runs through the site as an organizing element.

The foyer and dining area display the rich collection of materials and textures that characterize many of Cody's houses. The floor pattern by the door also edges the exterior walls of the entrance.

Although rectilinear in plan, the interior features curves in the conical fireplace and the barrel-vaulted ceiling, which seems to float above the clerestory windows.

The patterned concrete-block wall and complex pool shape are trademark Cody elements, while the concrete pavers duplicate the circles of the motor court.

The materials, textures, plantings, and vistas combine to create a rich, distinctive architectural experience.

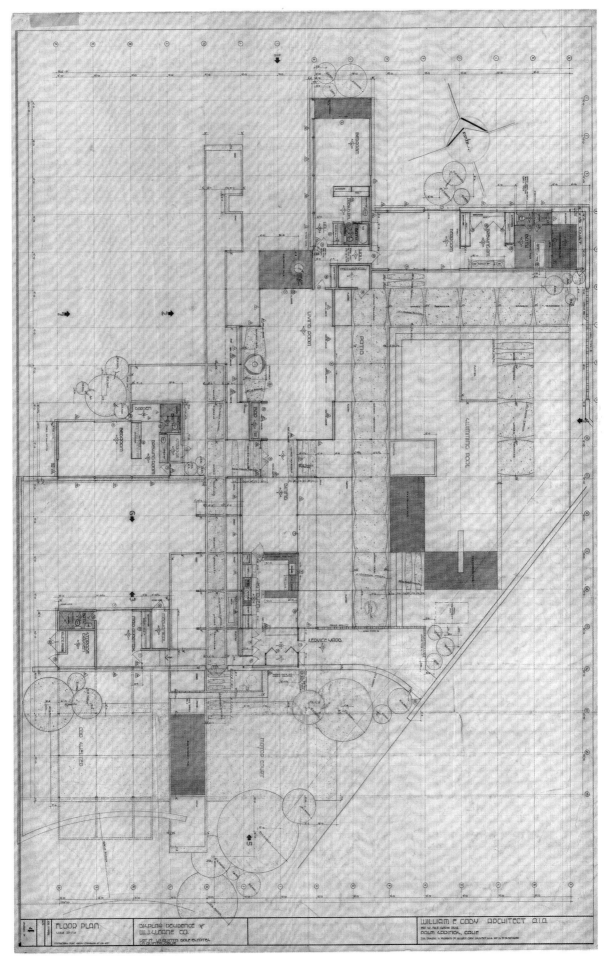

The floor plan shows a composition of wings extending outward from the entry, creating a dynamic pinwheel arrangement.

# Robert and Betty Cannon Residence

Indian Wells | California | 1961

Although Cody used wood for the structure of his early executed residential designs, he was also a master of steel construction, choosing materials based on the client, budget, and other circumstances. The strength of steel permitted very slender structural elements that allow openness and unobstructed views; this kind of spatial transparency is fundamental to the concept of fairway living as seen in the Cannon Residence and other homes that Cody designed for Eldorado Country Club Estates and other country clubs. Cody sited the Cannon Residence diagonally on the lot to capture views on three sides. To address the heat and sun of the Coachella Valley, the living areas, which face west toward the pool and links, are shaded by 12-foot-deep eaves. The bedrooms, which are oriented mainly toward the south, are effectively shaded during the summer by the deep overhangs. Air-conditioning was also provided.

Cody's strategic use of materials included wood, stone, and tile as well as steel. For example, he used square Spanish quarry tile to create a 90-foot-long circulation axis that begins outside with a breezeway in front of the house, continues through the entry and main living space, and extends outside again to the pool. The connection between living room and pool terrace is emphasized by the redwood siding of the ceiling, which extends from inside to outside as a continuous plane, interrupted only by the thin steel frames of the windows and sliding doors. The exposed face of each redwood board is milled to a concave section, giving the ceiling a subtle scalloped finish; the same siding is used for some interior and exterior walls as well. A massive wall and fireplace of Salton Sea stone anchors the living room, while teak veneer is used for cabinets and paneling. Colorful tile accents the service areas.

The Cannons built their house as a winter and weekend vacation home, and its layout embodies their preferred casual lifestyle. For instance, Cody combined the living, dining, and kitchen areas in one large, open space and also provided an informal, screen-roofed dining area off the kitchen. Maurice Martiné designed the interiors with a rich palette of colors and textures that complement Cody's sleek, modernist architecture.

The Cannon Residence was published in a four-page spread in the *Los Angeles Times Home Magazine* and was also featured in *House & Home* and *American Home*. The Southern California Chapter of the AIA recognized it with an Award of Merit, and it was selected by an international jury for the 1963 AIA Honor Awards Exhibition.

For the Cannon Residence pool, Cody eschewed a basic rectangle for a more expressive shape that matches the overall planning of the house.

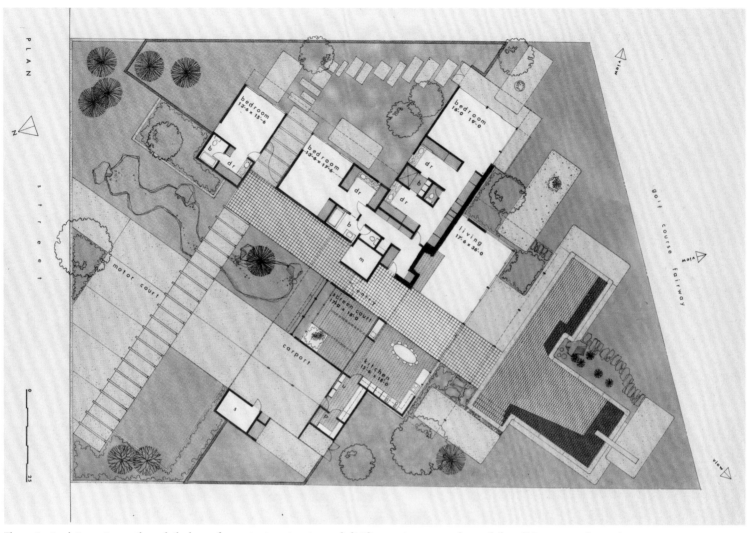

The main circulation axis runs through the house from entry to swimming pool, dividing service areas on the north from living areas to the south.

The low-arched concrete bridge repeats a form that Cody used at Eldorado Country Club and the Palm Springs Spa Hotel Bathhouse.

View from the southeast showing pool to left, living room in center, and primary bedroom to right.

The concrete walkway at left arches over a dry creek and extends through the breezeway that separates the guest casita from the main house.

For the living areas, Cody selected natural materials such as cupped redwood boards for the ceiling and local stone from the Salton Sea for the fireplace wall.

The kitchen, dining room, and living room share fairway, mountain, and pool views. Interior designer Maurice Martiné worked with Cody to select interior colors, materials, and finishes.

Sculptor Dale Clark designed the light fixture above the dining table.

# Desert Bel Air Estates

Indian Wells | California | 1961–64

Real estate developer Fillmore Crank developed Desert Bel Air Estates in Palm Desert (now Indian Wells) along with partners Robert Higgins and Robert Champion. Located just north of the Eldorado Country Club entrance, Desert Bel Air Estates encompassed 40 acres and over 100 homesites. Crank had previously commissioned Cody to design Tropicana Gardens, a residential development in Las Vegas, and in 1961 asked him to undertake a model home for his family directly across Fairway Drive from the Eldorado entrance. This house is a simple composition of two parallel volumes; one contains the living, dining, and kitchen areas, which are open to each other, and the other the bedrooms. The living room has full-height windows on three sides and looks out toward the west through a deep porch to the pool. Throughout the house, Cody used his trademark hush-and-flush window detail. The Crank-Garland House was remodeled by various owners over the decades, but after an extensive restoration by Jessy Moss and Steve Jocz, the city of Indian Wells designated it as local historical landmark no. 4 in 2019.

Cody designed a number of other model homes for Desert Bel Air Estates, including one called the Monterey that was described as "an unusual Romantic Spanish type home"; this house was a departure for Cody, with its "Spanish Mission plaster" walls and rough-hewn beams. It was purchased by interior designer Walter Dunivant and featured in *Architectural Digest* in 1968. Cody's final contribution to Desert Bel Air Estates was a group of six homes on the north side of Altamira Drive, completed in 1963 and 1964. One of these was purchased by John Cody (William Cody's brother) and his wife Elizabeth. Crank also commissioned a house from Cody in Paradise Valley, Arizona, in 1964.

At the first house Cody designed for Crank and Garland, a water feature and landscaping border the walkway to the front door. The two rectangular roof openings are mirrored in the roof beyond the entry hall.

A continuous fascia wraps around the house, integrating exterior spaces into the architecture. Visible to the left is the guest room.

The living room, pool terrace, kitchen, and dining area lie to the left of the entry, and the bedrooms to the right.

As in the W. & J. Sloane Display House, for this residence Cody designed a white conical fireplace in the living room.

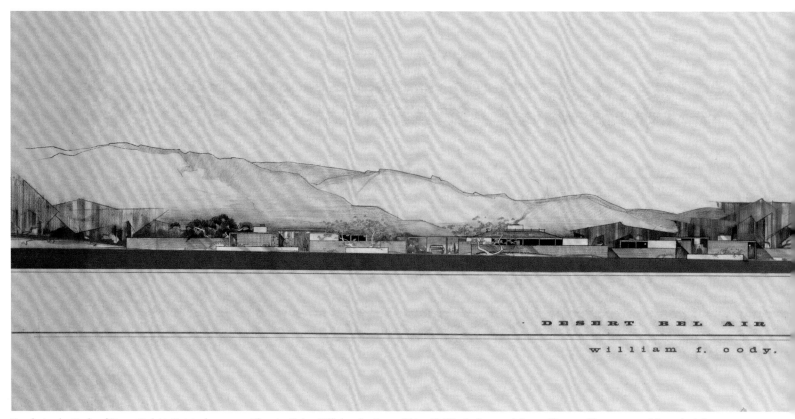

Rendering by Cody of Desert Bel Air Estates houses on Altamira Drive. Bill's brother Jay and his wife Elizabeth owned the pavilion-roof house, second from the left.

The Mr. & Mrs. W. Siemon Residence was one of six Desert Bel Air Estates homes designed by Cody on Altamira Drive.

FRONT ELEVATION

SCALE : ¼" = 1'-0"

J. LIEMON

□ □ □ ■

# Douglas Driggs Residence

Paradise Valley │ Arizona │ 1962

Douglas Driggs was president of Western Savings & Loan, which at the time was one of the largest savings and loan companies in Arizona. He asked Cody to design his home in Paradise Valley, a small, affluent town outside Phoenix. The house was sited on the fourth green of Paradise Valley Country Club's golf course, which was designed by Lawrence Hughes.

Given the climatic and geographic similarities between this Arizona site and the Coachella Valley, Cody employed many of his preferred elements, such as slender structure, glass walls, and deep overhangs. To take advantage of the dramatic site, at the Driggs Residence he created an open interior that allowed uninterrupted views through the house to the fairway on one side and to the swimming pool on the other; both enjoyed mountain views. The large living area comprised the living room and dining room, which were partially divided by a sculptural steel-and-wood screen designed by Cody. As in the Sloane Display House, Cody exposed the roof structure, using clerestory windows that made the ceiling appear to float above the living area. Tempered, heat-resistant glass flanked the fireplace, an element also seen at the Shamel Residence; here, it expanded the view from the living room to the fairway. The Driggs Residence has been razed.

The back of the house seen from the fairway.

Slender steel rafters project beyond the living room eaves and terminate in sawtooth patterns that evoke the mountain vistas.

Cody designed an open wood screen to divide the dining area from the living room.
On each side of the fireplace, tempered-glass windows allow views to the exterior.

The ends of the ceiling beams frame the clerestory windows of the living room.

The warm tones and horizontal lines of the brick wall contrast with the light-colored vertical wood siding and the dark mass of the living room chimney.

The architecture, pool, planters, and platforms create a complex, three-dimensional composition.

# Southridge Inc. Display House (Goldberg Residence)

Palm Springs | California | 1962

The vast majority of development in and around Palm Springs took place on the flatlands of the Coachella Valley, but in 1961 Southridge opened on the hillside south of town. This small, gated residential neighborhood was built at a higher elevation than any other development in the area and became home to celebrities such as Steve McQueen, William Holden, and Bob Hope, whose famous house by John Lautner crowns the development.

Cody designed a display house for Southridge Inc. that was purchased new by Chicago industrialist Stanley Goldberg and his wife. Like many wealthy home buyers in Palm Springs, the Goldbergs were cold-climate residents looking for informal living in a winter retreat. They chose frequent Cody collaborators Arthur Elrod and Harold Broderick as interior designers to help them complete a home for entertaining. (Incidentally, Elrod's own 1968 house in Southridge, designed by Lautner, became famous for its parties and its appearance in the 1971 James Bond film *Diamonds Are Forever.*)

For country club homes such as the Cannon Residence and Shamel Residence, Cody opened the house to views of the fairways and mountains. For the Goldberg Residence, he lined the entire north wall of the living room with floor-to-ceiling glass, allowing views over the pool toward Palm Springs and the valley. The adjoining east wall houses a fireplace and is covered with sumptuous walnut travertine, its opacity and pattern contrasting beautifully with the adjacent window wall. The table-height bar on the south wall of the living room serves as a focus for entertaining. Adjacent to the entry foyer, Cody placed a 12-by-20-foot glass-walled courtyard with a 6-foot-square pond, furthering the sense of transparency and the connection to the outdoors.

The current owners of the Goldberg Residence have deliberately restored many of the original interior design elements and have updated some areas with new flooring, countertops, and other materials. They have also changed the pool patio, rotating the pool 90 degrees.

The room with the piano was originally an exterior garden next to the dining room; it was later enclosed by the original owners of the house under the direction of Cody and Arthur Elrod. The front doors are also not original.

Pages 154 – 155: A fireplace and a walnut travertine wall anchor the living room, which originally could be separated by accordion doors from the study seen to the right of the stone wall.

The living room, entry, and dining room form a continuous space, with the kitchen seen in the background at right.

Southridge was the highest-elevation neighborhood in the Coachella Valley when built, guaranteeing exceptional views north over Palm Springs.

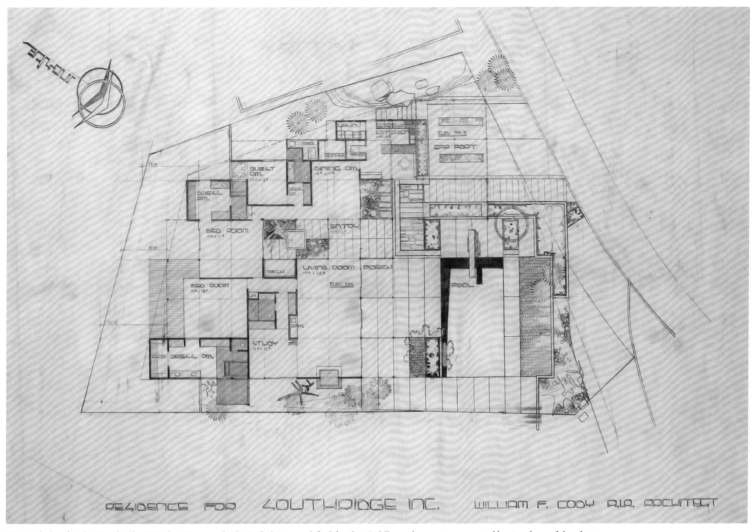

Original plan for the Southridge Display House, which Cody later modified for the Goldbergs by creating a seated bar in place of the closet and small bar shown here on the south side of the living room.

Detail of Cody's original presentation drawing (now lost), showing the house and pool terrace from the north.

# Western Savings & Loan

Tempe | Arizona | 1962

The Tempe branch of Western Savings & Loan was one of Cody's most eloquent statements in concrete. Designed with associated architect Alfred N. Beadle of Dailey Associates, it was simple in form—a set of rectangular volumes beneath a rectangular roof—but refined in detail and proportion. For instance, the columns had a subtle inverse taper, growing wider as they rose; graceful vertical indentations adorned the top third of each face of the columns. The columns also served as the visual framework of the building, standing out against the darker walls of textured masonry or tinted glass. Cody set the walls inside the outer face of the columns, separating the masonry walls from the columns with narrow bands of glass. He also opened slots in the roof at the column tops, creating a rhythm of bright openings under the eaves. The roof's slightly rounded corners and beveled eaves added to its elegance and visual lightness.

Although unequivocally a modern building in form and material, the bank's clear outline, graceful columns, and overall proportions also suggested affinities with classical temples, which were themselves common inspirations for bank buildings through the early twentieth century. The front end of the bank even had a columned porch analogous to the portico of a typical ancient Roman temple. In contrast, the back end consisted of a glass volume elevated off the ground, an archetypal modernist composition. The serene coexistence of classical allusions and modernist conventions spoke of Cody's talent in synthesizing various influences into a rich and highly distinctive design.

The geometric patterns and textures of the walls contrast with the smooth white plane of the roof.

The concrete frame and thin profile of the roof stand out when seen from the side street, their connection emphasized by the slots in the roof at the column tops.

A columned porch adorns the short facade, not unlike the composition of a classical temple.

The back of the bank houses an elevated glass box with parking underneath.

# Palm Springs Spa Hotel

Palm Springs  |  California  |  1963

After the successful completion of the Palm Springs Spa in 1959, Banowit and Cody turned their attention to building the Palm Springs Spa Hotel, the second phase of construction on the site. The hotel posed a major risk: even a twenty-five-year lease as allowed under existing law was too short to justify the large investment Banowit planned. More generally, short leases prevented the Agua Caliente Band of Cahuilla Indians from developing and profiting from their land, some of which was located in the heart of Palm Springs.

In order to secure greater control of their property, Vyola Ortner, who in 1954 became the chair of the tribal council—at the time the first all-female tribal council in the nation—and her colleagues commenced frequent lobbying trips to Washington D.C. Palm Springs mayor Frank Bogert and real estate executives Russell Wade and Lew Levy also participated in this work, knowing that development of Section 14 would prove profitable to the city and private developers, as well as to the Agua Caliente Band. The efforts of Ortner and her allies culminated in Public Law 86-326, approved by Congress on September 21, 1959, which secured the right to grant ninety-nine-year leases for Agua Caliente lands only; all other reservations continued to be limited to twenty-five-year leases.

Cody's office expanded for the design and construction of the hotel, allowing him take full responsibility for design, project management, and construction documentation, although Philip Koenig served as Banowit's representative as he had for the spa project. Albert Parvin & Co. designed custom furniture for the lobby and guest rooms. Completed in 1963, the Palm Springs Spa Hotel was one of the city's earliest steel and reinforced-concrete hotels. It provided 131 guest rooms, dining, a gym, a meeting room, shops, and other facilities in addition to its own swimming pool. Two additional floors, containing 102 units, were added in 1965. The Spa Hotel was touted as "the healthiest hotel in the world," thanks to the qualities of the spa's waters and the warmth of the desert sun.

As with the bathhouse, for the hotel Cody designed a dramatic entry, creating a slender, graceful canopy to serve as a porte cochère. A basic T-shape in plan, the building's exterior was enlivened by balconies on the west side facing the pool and by combinations of vertical and horizontal window on the east side. Inside, the guest rooms were bright and simply decorated with modern, wood furniture. As in other Cody-designed hotels in Palm Springs, such as the Del Marcos Apartment Hotel and L'Horizon Hotel, the focus was on leisure and entertainment in a casual but refined setting.

The balconies on the main wing of the hotel offer outstanding pool and mountain views.

View from the south of the hotel pool and the guest rooms of the main wing.

The south wing of the hotel, showing its unique fenestration. The entrance to the bathhouse is at the right end of the wing.

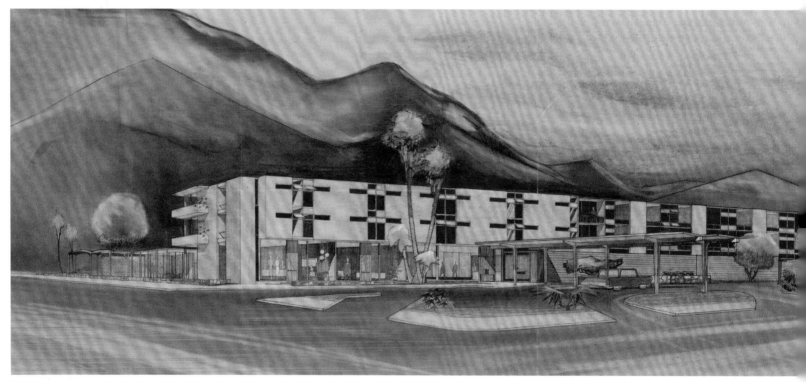

For the executed project, Cody modified the porte-cochere and certain other elements from the preliminary design shown in his presentation drawing.

For the hotel entry, Cody designed an angular porte-cochere that contrasts with the bathhouse's arched canopy.

Seen from the porte-cochere, the fenestration of the guest rooms above the ground-floor boutiques
enlivens the simple form of the hotel's main wing.

Equipped with kitchens and dining areas, some guest room suites functioned as complete apartments.

Bold colors in the furniture and carpeting accent the bright hotel lobby.

In the Agua Room lounge and bar, the ceiling's articulation is as important as the interior design to create distinct areas.

# Jennings B. and Anna Shamel Residence

Indian Wells │ California │ 1963

Like many homeowners in the Eldorado Country Club development, Jennings and Anna Shamel built their fairway home as a winter residence for relaxed living and recreation, notably golf.

On a lot bordered on three sides by the tenth and thirteenth fairways, Cody created multiple layers of space to guarantee privacy without sacrificing the clients' desire for an open, informal interior. The slender structure of the house, composed of 4-inch-square steel columns on a 12-by-12-foot grid, was all but invisible, allowing Cody maximum flexibility in planning.

The screen-covered entry court at the core of the house served as a sheltered, semi-outdoor room and also provided access to the bedroom, living, and service zones. On the west side of the house, a portico offered protection from the afternoon sun while also creating a buffer between the fairway and the glass-walled living room. As mandated by Eldorado's bylaws, no barriers were permitted between the house and the fairways—a stipulation that Cody had first introduced for the master plan at Thunderbird Country Club—which allowed exceptional views of the golf course and mountains. The roof appeared to float above the interior, supported by slender columns and extending outward to frame views and provide shade.

Throughout the house, Cody designed distinctive details, ranging from the direct-set glass of the kitchen windows to the entry lamp beside the front door. Interior materials such as teak, travertine, slate, and indigenous stone created rich textures and warm colors that contrasted with the steel columns and large areas of glass. The living room fireplace in particular showed off this strategic juxtaposition of materials: four panels of travertine hovered above the fireplace opening, while the rough stone wall in the background could be seen through the tempered glass that filled in the space between the steel columns and the fireplace.

The Shamel Residence was one of Cody's most widely recognized residential projects, featured in the *Los Angeles Times* and *Architecture/West*, among other publications. It was also chosen as one of eleven winners of the 1965 American Institute of Steel Construction Architectural Awards of Excellence. The award jurors wrote, "its design reflects the infinite variety of life that takes places (sic) in a house of this kind. It is an unpretentious and straightforward solution to a beautiful location—simple, direct, straight to the point." The Shamel Residence also garnered a 1964 Homes for Better Living award from the AIA. Unfortunately, the house has been razed and the lot remains empty.

The roof structure protects the interior from direct sun and provides shade over the patio, pocket gardens, and part of the pool.

The steps and landing are integrated with the pools and planters. Cody designed the sculptural exterior light fixture next to the entrance doors as a housewarming gift for the Shamels.

Motor court and front entrance, showing the fieldstone wall juxtaposed with wood beams, steel columns, and stucco walls.

The back of the house faces the tenth and thirteenth fairways, without architectural features to interrupt the views of Eldorado's golf course and the mountains beyond.

The entry court, partially roofed with screening, can be opened to the living areas through the full-height glass doors seen to the left. The front door is at center-left, and behind the stone wall are the primary bedroom suite and another bedroom.

The pool extends under the entry wall to the exterior, similar to the pool at the Palm Springs Spa bathhouse.

Matched paneling is used throughout the kitchen and dining room to form continuous planes of beautifully grained wood. The glass of the kitchen windows extends directly into the ceiling above and countertop below, eliminating visual obstructions between inside and outside.

The glass doors of the dining area lead to a covered walkway that connects with the poolside patio. As in other parts of the house, the orientation of the ceiling boards alternates with each bay.

Outside the living room, a palm tree grows through an opening in the roof.

The living room fireplace is faced with travertine and flanked by glass. In front of the fireplace, the slate floor is dropped to create an intimate seating area.

Seen from just inside the front door, the fireplace and a garden separate the living room on the left from the stone wall of the primary bedroom to the right.

# James and Helen Abernathy Residence

Palm Springs | California | 1963

Although Cody's steel designs of the early 1960s may have been more widely publicized, his house for Helen and James Logan Abernathy is a reminder that he was no less creative when working in wood. On the exterior, most striking are the pyramidal and hipped roofs covered with wooden shakes—both the forms and the rough texture are unusual in Cody's oeuvre and in modernist buildings in general. Each of the four hipped roofs identifies one of the house's wings, while the pyramidal roof crowns the living room at the building's core.

Above its terrazzo floor, the living room is essentially a pavilion of wood and glass: laminated beams rise from the perimeter to form the hovering pyramidal roof structure, while tongue-in-groove decking forms the ceiling and siding covers two walls; the other two walls comprise floor-to-ceiling glass.

All of the major rooms boast exterior patios, while gardens and planters are interspersed throughout the plan. In the primary bathroom, the terrazzo floor extends outside into a private courtyard, where an oval-shaped planting area echoes the shape of the sunken tub inside.

At first glance, the overall layout of the house resembles a modernist pinwheel plan, with wings spiraling out from the living room. In fact, though, the interior spaces are relatively clearly defined, unlike the flowing spaces of many other modernist designs, including Cody's

contemporaneous Shamel House. For instance, four planes—albeit some of them transparent—define the living room and primary bedroom as enclosed squares. Spatially, then, the Abernathy Residence is a kind of hybrid, one that may have roots as far back as the rambling ranch-house plans that Cody produced with Cliff May in the late 1930s.

The house was planned to meet the particular needs of the clients, who desired a home for their retirement years with only one bedroom (plus a maid's room) but with generous entertaining areas, including the spacious, high-ceilinged living room and extensive outdoor spaces. For Helen, a co-founder of the Palm Springs Civic Art Association and a well-known painter, Cody provided a studio with a north wall of floor-to-ceiling glass to secure even light.

Although many of the elements of the design were based on Helen's artistic and social activities, she unfortunately had little chance to use them, passing away in August 1963. James married Magdalen (Madge) Phillips, also a painter, in December 1964 and they lived in the house until his death in 1980; Madge remained until 1991, when she sold to the noted interior designer Hal Broderick. The Abernathy Residence has been sensitively modified, restored, and updated and in 2013 was designated as a Class 1 Historic Site by the city of Palm Springs.

View from the corner of the primary bedroom wing over the pool toward the living, dining, and kitchen areas. (*Palm Springs Life* stamped on the back)

From left, the living room pavilion, the slump block exterior wall of the dressing room, and the primary bedroom.

View of the breakfast and dining areas to the left and the living room to the right; all of these spaces boast generous patios. (*Palm Springs Life* stamped on the back)

View from the living room toward the pool, garden, and Mount San Jacinto.

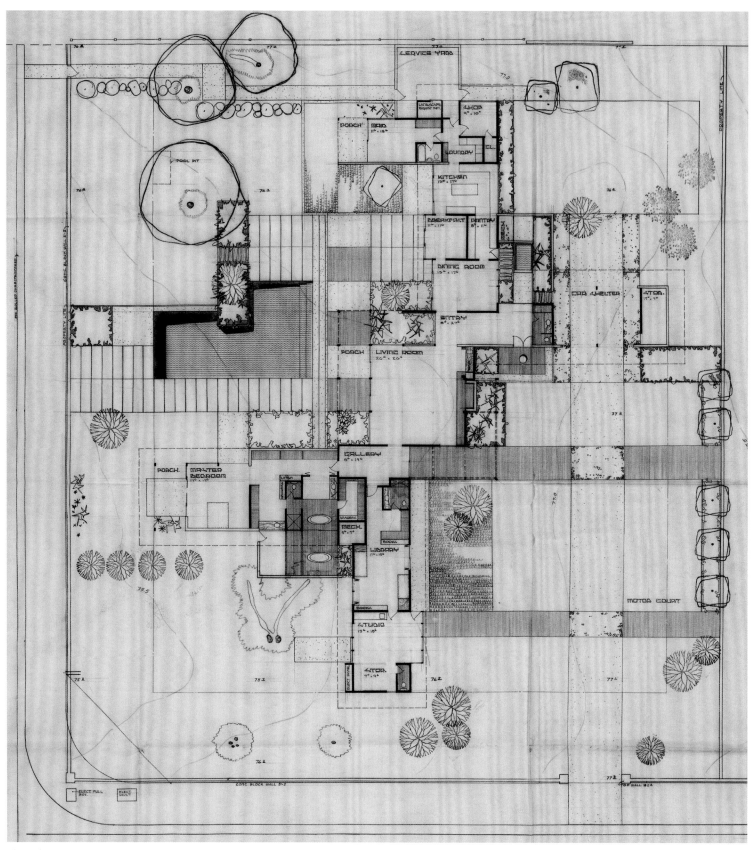

Floor plan oriented with north to the right, showing the four wings—dining/kitchen/maid's room, carport, library/studio, primary bedroom suite—radiating from the central living room.

View from the motor court showing the studio at left and the living-room chimney at right.

View from the carport toward the back of the living room, with the main entrance down the shallow steps to the right. (no stamp on the back, though likely taken at the same time as the two from PSL)

# Palm Springs Tennis Club Projects

Palm Springs | California | 1963–73

Harry Chaddick, a prominent Chicago entrepreneur and developer, was yet another ambitious client who commissioned Cody for several large-scale projects, beginning with Palm Springs Tennis Club and continuing with Whitewater Country Club and a new luxury residential neighborhood called Andreas Hills. Although golf was the most important sport in establishing the Palm Springs area as a recreation destination, tennis played a major role as well. The earliest major tennis clubs were the Racquet Club, founded in 1934, and the Palm Springs Tennis Club, which opened in 1938. Top players such as Alice Marble, Fred Perry, Don Budge, and Jack Kramer frequented these venues for tournaments, exhibition matches, and recreation. In comparison with the Racquet Club, which was famous for its Hollywood connections, the Tennis Club was more genteel and perhaps even more monied.

The Tennis Club's original buildings were designed by Philip G. Ormsby and Lloyd Steffgen to evoke an old-world atmosphere, but it was the 1947 clubhouse and cocktail lounge by Paul R. Williams and A. Quincy Jones, who was one of Cody's closest friends, that turned the club into what *The Desert Sun* called, perhaps rather parochially, the "most beautiful Club in America, if not the world." Certainly, their spare, clean forms contrasted dramatically with the lush landscaping and the dramatic desert site. Like Cody's

Del Marcos Hotel, the new Tennis Club architecture embodied the application of modernist principles to the desert's cultural and geographical context.

By the time Chaddick bought the Palm Springs Tennis Club in 1961, he had already founded and sold American Transportation Company, one of the nation's largest trucking companies, before turning his attention to real estate. Although his largest projects, such as Ford City shopping center, were in Chicago, he also became the most active developer in Palm Springs. By 1975 he had developed about 1,000 acres, leading *The Desert Sun* to call him "the largest single investor in the history of Palm Springs." After purchasing the Palm Springs Tennis Club from its founder Pearl McManus, Chaddick made major renovations to update and expand the club, hiring Cody to work on a series of projects. The first was a set of more than twenty bungalows, commissioned in 1962 and completed the following year across the street just northeast of the clubhouse. In 1964, Cody designed an additional group of bungalows on the adjoining property to the east. All of the bungalows were provided with housekeeping, switchboard service, and room service.

In 1963, Cody designed condominium units directly south and east of the clubhouse for what Chaddick called "The Tennis Club Homes"; fifty units were planned, although it is unclear if all were executed.

The color and texture of the split-face concrete blocks used in the construction complement the rugged mountain behind.

Palm trees flank the hotel entry, which leads to a grand, two-story lobby.

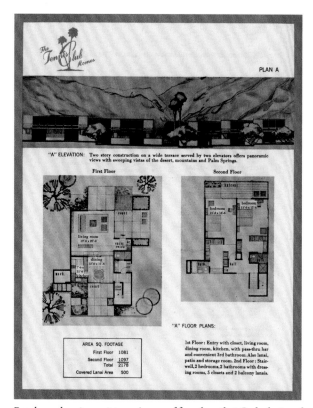

Brochure showing unit type A, one of five plans that Cody designed for the complex. The two-story A-unit boasted views of the landscape and city of Palm Springs.

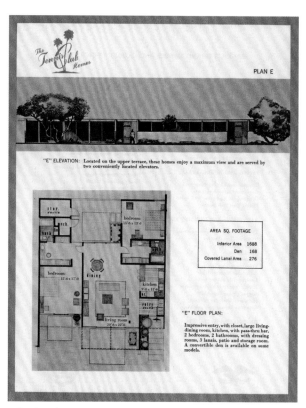

Like the other unit types, type E was designed with open living areas and shaded patio spaces for casual, convenient living.

As with the earlier bungalows, buyers of the Tennis Club Homes enjoyed Tennis Club privileges as well as maid, maintenance, and switchboard services. Compared with the Cottages West project that Cody had designed for the Racquet Club, the Tennis Club condominium development was larger and more luxurious, its units intended for long-term residence. Cody designed five different unit types, each with two bedrooms; most buildings were single-story, ranging from 1,605 to 1,757 square feet, but the largest type was two stories and encompassed 2,178 square feet. Arthur Elrod furnished the development's model home. With their floor-to-ceiling glass and clean rectangular forms, the Tennis Club Homes display a simple, modern elegance that contrasts with the rugged hillside looming immediately to the west. Although the high density of the units required a conditional use permit (the land was zoned R-1A for single-family residences) and provoked some controversy, Chaddick broke ground on the project in February 1965. Along with the earlier fifty-two bungalows, the Tennis Club Homes transformed the Palm Springs Tennis Club from a recreational facility into a full-fledged community, a shift that paralleled the creation of golf club communities such as Eldorado Country Club.

In 1969, Chaddick announced the purchase of the McManus estate directly north of the Tennis Club, stating his plans to erect a ten-story, 200-room hotel on the site at the base of 10,834-foot Mount San Jacinto. Two years later, he formally proposed a six-story hotel with 150 rooms, but even this smaller project ran afoul of the city's zoning regulations, which defined the site as R-2 (multifamily residential). Ultimately, Chaddick and Cody produced a two-story luxury hotel for which no zoning concessions were needed. In addition to 105 guest rooms, the hotel included a monumental lobby, meeting rooms, two pools, and an underground parking lot accommodating 100 cars. It was completed in November 1973.

Forced by the shape of the lot to design a long, narrow building, Cody staggered the sections, using setbacks and projecting walls to break up the hotel's 600-foot length. He paid close attention to the landscaping, using palms, lawns, and other vegetation to create the sense of an oasis at the foot of the mountains. Instead of conventional corridors, visitors traverse breezeways lined with large planters to reach their rooms. For the structural walls, Cody chose beige-colored split face concrete block whose desert color and rugged texture match the mountain beyond; these walls are exposed inside the guest rooms as well as on the exterior. Geographically and architecturally, the hotel serves as an intermediary between the single-story Tennis Club bungalows to its east and the monumental natural backdrop of Mount San Jacinto to its west.

The Phase 1 bungalows on Baristo Road and S. Tahquitz Drive are oriented toward interior green spaces to form a resort community.

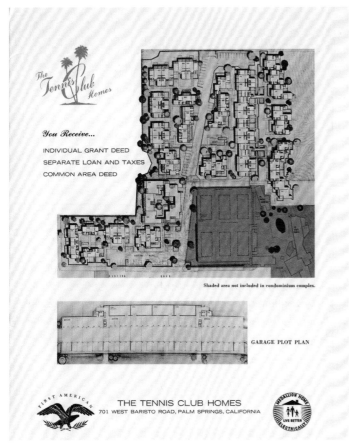

Promotional brochure for the Tennis Club Homes to be built east and south of the clubhouse.

Harry Chaddick and William Cody photographed on October 28, 1964, for the Tennis Club Homes groundbreaking.

# Western Savings & Loan Home Office

Phoenix | Arizona | 1964

Western Savings & Loan commissioned two offices from Cody, one in Tempe and the other in Phoenix. Although he had used concrete to strong effect for the branch office in Tempe, for the home office in Phoenix, Cody designed a 4,500-square-foot steel-and-glass building. As with the Western Savings & Loan Tempe branch, Alfred N. Beadle of Dailey Associates served as associated architect. Of all of Cody's buildings, the Western Savings & Loan Home Office was the one most closely aligned with the corporate modernism of the 1950s and '60s. An alternate design shows walls and arcades with gentle arches like the ones of the Nicoletti Residence in Rancho Mirage, but the executed building is a clean, symmetric steel structure reminiscent of the work of Mies van der Rohe. A shallow set of stairs leads to a recessed entry, offering a suggestion of ceremony that helped make this building more than just an anonymous, elevated box.

This building was recognized in 1965 by the American Iron and Steel Institute for architectural excellence in low-rise commercial construction and by the American Institute of Steel Construction for outstanding aesthetic design in steel-framed construction. It also received a Valley Beautiful Award in 1966 from the Valley Beautiful Council in Arizona. After Western Savings & Loan moved to the Phoenix Financial Center, the building was moved to a new location on Seventh Avenue, where it remains recognizable under considerable alterations.

The dark volume of the Western Savings & Loan home office seems to float above the ground.

Approaching the recessed entrance, broad, shallow steps lead to a landing with diagonal steel stays. A row of white circular planters contrasts with the lines and dark color of the building.

The clean details of the projecting window wall show Cody's close attention to design, crucial in a building as unadorned as this one.

A dark box by day, the bank glows through its floor-to-ceiling glass in the evening. The floor and the ceiling materials continue from outside to inside, drawing in visitors.

Open at both ends, the lobby extends through the center of the building.

# Valley Wide Center Master Plan

Palm Desert | California | 1964 (unbuilt)

Although best known for residences and leisure facilities, Cody also designed a number of commercial projects, for instance the Cameron Center in Palm Springs and the Hi Fidelity complex in Menlo Park. The master plan for Valley Wide Center in Palm Desert was on a far larger scale than these earlier projects, though, encompassing 25 acres and thirty buildings for commercial, retail, and professional clients. The development was headed by Cody, real estate executive Russell Wade, and industrialists Robert P. McCulloch and Robert Cannon, all of whom had previously worked with Cody.

Cody and his partners imagined Valley Wide Center as an urban hub that would help establish Palm Desert as the center of the region. Unlike most commercial developments in the area, Valley Wide Center was conceived not as a strip mall along a road but as a kind of commercial neighborhood with various types of buildings and amenities. Cody stated, "no part of Valley Wide Center will face Highway 111. It will be turned inward, upon itself, with cool pools and dancing fountains, sparkling tree-shaded malls." Seventy percent of the parking would be covered, a great boon in the triple-digit temperatures of the warmer months. Phase 1, east of the highway, was planned to include a supermarket, a building for medical professionals, an

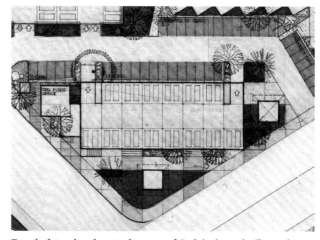

Detail of site plan showing location of Cody's planned office at the intersection of Park View Drive and Highway 111.

office building, and other stores. Cody's firm, Cody & Associates, planned to occupy 35 percent of a two-story, 12,500-square-foot office building to be owned by Cody. The proposal for phase 2, to the west, contained a six-story hotel, department stores, and merchandise marts. The Valley Wide Center was not executed.

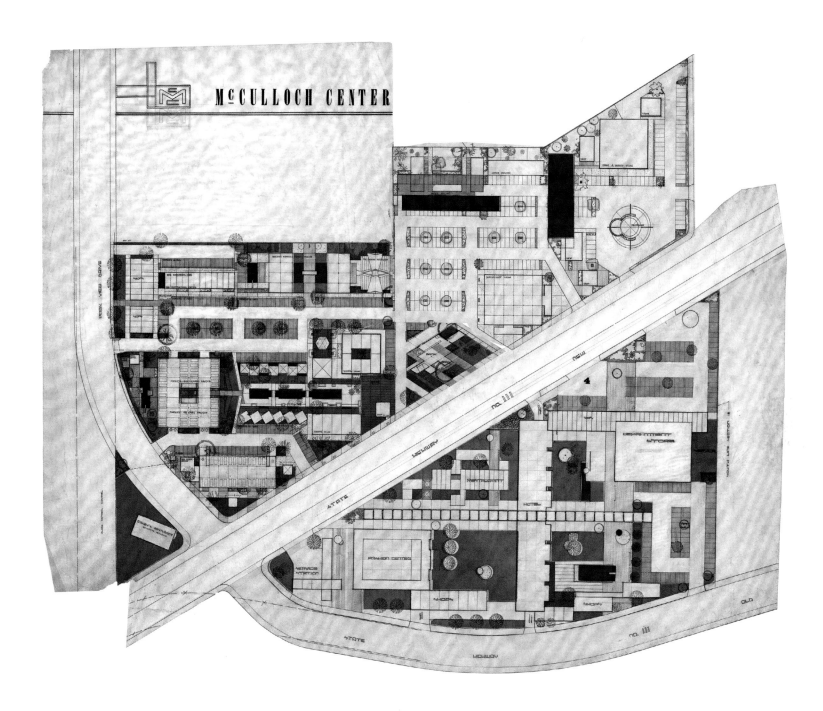

Unlike most large-scale commercial developments of the time, the Valley Wide Center on Highway 111 in Palm Desert was planned to include a large range of functions, spaces, and scales, including large department stores, small shops, offices, and a hotel.

# Weir McDonald Residence

Paradise Valley | Arizona | 1965

Like the Driggs Residence of a few years earlier, the McDonald Residence was built along the links of the Paradise Valley Country Club. Standing on a small rise on a lot of almost 2 acres, it is one of Cody's most strikingly three-dimensional houses. Planters line a series of steps and ramps that lead up to the entry courtyard. To the left, a simple rectangular volume containing garage and storage floats above the slope. Unlike typical Cody designs in the Coachella Valley, much of the McDonald Residence is raised above the ground on steel columns; the house and its structure seem exceptionally light even by Cody's standards. Steel framing extends beyond the house to encompass a saguaro cactus and palm trees. The siting takes advantage of exceptional views toward Mummy Mountain to the east and Camelback Mountain to the south.

The complex plan of the house is organized on a simple, 10-foot-square grid, which is visible in the spacing of the columns and most walls. Inside, the main living spaces are the living room and trophy room, both measuring 40 by 20 feet. An office/guest suite lies between the trophy room and garage wing, and a separate guest suite is located at the south end of the house. The trophy room is an anomaly in Cody's

work: a solid, windowless rectangle lined in hardwood-veneer plywood, it was used by the original owner to display game trophies and also as a projection room—a retractable screen was hidden in the ceiling at one end of the room.

The Paradise Valley Country Club remains one of Arizona's most prestigious country clubs, and the McDonald Residence stands today in excellent condition, albeit with significant interior remodeling. It has been refurbished by the current owners.

Vintage photo showing the entry approach, with elevated garage to left of walkway and detached guest quarters at far right.

Adobe planters, ground beds, and steel frames offer a variety of settings for plantings.

The full-height door and side light are familiar Cody motifs, as is the terrazzo floor that continues to the exterior.

A covered walkway steps down along the front side of the house and terminates at the detached guesthouse.

View toward the primary bath and bedroom, with a saguaro framed by steel members.

View from the primary bedroom of the pool (not original), golf course, and Camelback Mountain.

View from the living room showing the terrace, bedroom, and steel roof frames.

# Dr. Branch and Carol Kerfoot Residence

Newport Beach | California | 1967

In most of the residences he designed in and around Palm Springs, Cody emphasized horizontal lines; these one-story houses expanded into the landscape, fitting perfectly into a wide-open terrain that had few tall buildings. In contrast, the most distinctive space in the Kerfoot Residence in Newport Beach is the spacious two-story living room that welcomes visitors immediately upon entry. This is a different vision of modern, casual living, one that revolves around the clients' love of art. The 16-foot-high walls of the living room offer ample space for hanging paintings, while floor-to-ceiling windows on three walls provide bright, even lighting. For Carol Saindon Kerfoot, an artist, Cody designed a second-floor studio overlooking the living room. With wall-to-wall windows facing north to the exterior and west to the living room, as well as windows to the covered balcony to the east, the studio enjoys even, indirect light almost regardless of exterior conditions.

Most of the finish materials in the Kerfoot Residence are relatively modest, but as usual Cody used them strategically. For example, the vertical wood siding of living room interior "folds" horizontally to become the ceiling of the dining room, helping integrate the two spaces. In fact, there are no conventional doorways in the living room; instead, the openings to the dining room, library, and hallway are unframed and extend up to the 8-foot ceiling height. In several places, Cody chose more luxurious materials for emphasis. One was the entry, where he used two, 8-foot-tall walnut doors, with escutcheons of his own design on the exterior. The grain of the wood extends to the 8-foot panels above the doors, forming a continuous, two-story walnut wall. The other point of emphasis in the living room is the fireplace: the simple marble mantelpiece imitates the frame of a painting and is complemented by a shelf of the same stone beneath.

The Kerfoot Residence is also remarkable for its condition: in residence for over fifty years, the original owner has made no changes to the architecture. She recalls the building process fondly: "My husband and I loved working with Bill Cody as his designs took shape. Branch and I were both involved in the process but certainly gave Bill his lead. We counted Bill a friend and greatly admired his work, his discipline, vision and integrity."

Evening lighting shows off the double-height living room, glazed garden wall, and the custom doors of the three-car garage, which Cody provided to house Branch Kerfoot's classic car collection.

Pages 202 – 203: The entry walkway leads to a 16-foot-high surface of walnut veneer comprising a pair of 8-foot doors surmounted by 8-foot panels. A sculpture by Michael Todd casts a shadow on the opaque glass of the entry garden wall.

The cedar siding of the living room extends to the ceiling plane of the dining room. Both the dining room and kitchen beyond have views of the entry garden.

The living room was intended to display art, and the marble fireplace surround even mimics a picture frame. In the background are the library and second-floor art studio, which is open on three sides for natural light.

The quarry tile entry axis continues inside and leads to the family room at the rear of the house. Seen at left are the accordion doors of the den, which match the siding of the walls.

Pages 206 – 207: From the backyard, the art studio is above the den on the right, and the family room is on the left.

# Rhu House, Lemurian Fellowship

Ramona | California | 1968

In 1956, Maurice Martiné introduced Cody to Bill Elliot, the representative for the Lemurian Fellowship, a spiritual community near Ramona, California. The fellowship included a number of talented woodworkers, potters, and metalworkers; Reynolds G. Dennis, for example, designed a black walnut beaker that was acquired by New York's Museum of Modern Art and shown at two exhibitions in 1951–52 and 1958–59. Of more direct interest to Cody was the modern architectural hardware that the Lemurian Fellowship produced, notably door pulls and push plates. He began commissioning the fellowship to fabricate his own custom door hardware, which led to commissions from the group to remodel its existing buildings and design new ones.

Cody's designs for the Lemurians included Rhu House, which is the community center, as well as parking areas and landscaping. Although the alterations and additions to existing buildings were completed in 1958, it took many years for the fellowship to raise the funds to build Rhu House, but Dennis, who had become the fellowship spokesperson, requested that the project be built to Cody's original design.

Members of the fellowship related to Cody that the equilateral triangle was an important symbol for the Lemurians, the three sides representing mentality, ideality, and materiality—the three essential aspects of balance. Cody thus chose the 60-degree angle as the basis of his design for Rhu House; in fact, his previous experience using acute angles in projects such as L'Horizon Hotel and The Springs restaurant may have been a factor in the Lemurian Fellowship choosing him as its architect. In its use of fieldstone and exposed wood, Rhu House also resembles the Del Marcos Apartment Hotel, another Cody design that used non-orthogonal angles. Triangles appear throughout the Lemurian Fellowship buildings and landscape, from exterior stone walls to roof forms to the exquisite copper fireplace. The stone came from the Chocolate Mountains near Twentynine Palms.

The angle of the Rhu House roof echoes the slopes of the surrounding valleys and mountains.

Stone was selected from the Chocolate Mountains near Twentynine Palms to harmonize with the natural surroundings.

The roof plane in the community room appears to hover above the glass, an effect heightened by Cody's hush-and-flush treatment in which the glass pane connects to the ceiling without any projecting frames or moldings.

The frame of the pool continues to the interior to form the triangular base of the fireplace.

The mouth of the angular, flaring chimney hood rests above a triangular firepit which extends from the exterior pool. The fireplace was fabricated by Barney Mitchell of Ransom Bros. Sheet Metal.

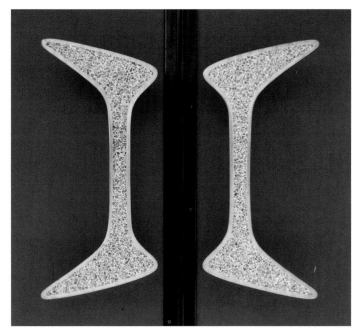

Many of Cody's door hardware and cabinet pull designs, such as these pulls for Eldorado Country Club, were fabricated in stone inlay and metal by artisans at the Lemurian Fellowship.

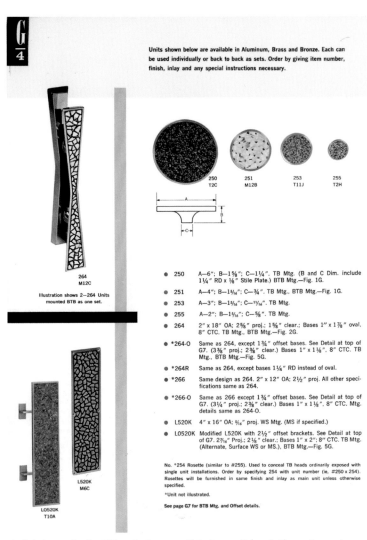

G/4

Units shown below are available in Aluminum, Brass and Bronze. Each can be used individually or back to back as sets. Order by giving item number, finish, inlay and any special instructions necessary.

250
T2C

251
M12B

253
T11J

255
T2H

264
M12C

Illustration shows 2—264 Units mounted BTB as one set.

L520K
M6C

LO520K
T10A

● 250   A—6"; B—1⅝"; C—1¼". TB Mtg. (B and C Dim. include 1¼" RD x ⅛" Stile Plate.) BTB Mtg.—Fig. 1G.

● 251   A—4"; B—1⁵⁄₁₆"; C—¾". TB Mtg., BTB Mtg.—Fig. 1G.

● 253   A—3"; B—1⁵⁄₁₆"; C—¹¹⁄₁₆". TB Mtg.

● 255   A—2"; B—1⁵⁄₁₆"; C—⅝". TB Mtg.

● 264   2" x 18" OA; 2⅜" proj.; 1⅝" clear.; Bases 1" x 1⅞" oval. 8" CTC. TB Mtg., BTB Mtg.—Fig. 2G.

● *264-O   Same as 264, except 1¾" offset bases. See Detail at top of G7. (3⅜" proj.; 2⅜" clear.) Bases 1" x 1⅛". 8" CTC. TB Mtg., BTB Mtg.—Fig. 5G.

● *264R   Same as 264, except bases 1¼" RD instead of oval.

● *266   Same design as 264. 2" x 12" OA; 2½" proj. All other specifications same as 264.

● *266-O   Same as 266 except 1¾" offset bases. See Detail at top of G7. (3¼" proj.; 2⅜" clear.) Bases 1" x 1⅛". 8" CTC. Mtg. details same as 264-O.

● L520K   4" x 16" OA; ⁵⁄₁₆" proj. WS Mtg. (MS if specified.)

● LO520K   Modified L520K with 2½" offset brackets. See Detail at top of G7. 2⁷⁄₁₆" Proj.; 2⅛" clear.; Bases 1" x 2"; 8" CTC. TB Mtg. (Alternate, Surface WS or MS.), BTB Mtg.—Fig. 5G.

No. *254 Rosette (similar to #255). Used to conceal TB heads ordinarily exposed with single unit installations. Order by specifying 254 with unit number (ie, #250 x 254). Rosettes will be furnished in same finish and inlay as main unit unless otherwise specified.

*Unit not illustrated.

See page G7 for BTB Mtg. and Offset details.

Cody's design for the Eldorado Country Club door pull (top left) was featured in the Lemurian Fellowship's product catalog. A slightly modified version, dubbed the "WC" for William Cody, sold well during its dozen-year run.

Expressive, tightly paired columns support the breezeway.

Cody drawing of Rhu House, 1965.

Aerial view of Rhu House showing 60-degree angles in plan. Google Earth, Image 2020 Landsat / Copernicus.

# St. Theresa
# Catholic Church

Palm Springs  |  California  |  1968

Dedicated on Thanksgiving Day, 1968, St. Theresa Church, the Cody family's parish church, is perhaps the greatest testament to the depth and breadth of Cody's talents. It was at once an intensely personal work and a strongly collaborative one for Cody: although he designed the architecture down to the smallest details, the overall effect of the church depended also on the high quality of the furnishings and artworks produced by others. In 1963, Cody produced a master plan for the complex, which included a church, convent, school, and rectory. Bob Hope was the major donor for the convent, which was completed in 1965.

For Cody and St. Theresa parish, the design of the church required exceptional consideration, as shown in both an early, angular, concrete proposal and the final, timber-framed building. One reason was simply that the project was unique in Cody's career. He had designed a number of religious projects early in his career, including Village Church of the West in Phoenix (1948; designed with Phoenix architect and fellow USC graduate Ralph Haver), Our Lady of Malibu Catholic Church (1949), and a chapel for Mercer Mortuary in Phoenix (1950). However, a modest alteration for St. Louis Church in Cathedral City (1958) notwithstanding, Cody did not have the opportunity to

design a major church project in the Coachella Valley until St. Theresa. Given that Cody chose to design every element of the church himself rather than relying on historical designs or off-the-shelf elements, the process inevitably required considerable time.

Another factor that encouraged Cody to think deeply about his design was the Second Vatican Council of 1962–65, especially its implications for buildings, art, and furnishings. For architects in particular, the new call for active participation seemed particularly relevant: "Mother Church earnestly desires that all the faithful should be led to that fully conscious, (sic) and active participation in liturgical celebrations which is demanded by the very nature of the liturgy." Many designers and church leaders took this to mean that the congregation should be seated as close as possible to the altar. In St. Theresa, Cody designed the sanctuary to be four steps above the main floor and surrounded on three sides by the nave and transept, both of equal breadth; this allowed members of congregation close proximity and good sight lines to major rituals.

The Second Vatican Council also stated support for modern art: "The art of our own days, coming from every race and region, shall also be given free scope

At the front entrance, two pairs of doors are sheltered by a canopy whose curved wooden supports play off the forms of the concrete walls.

PROPOSED CH RCH FOR ST. THERESA PARISH ·
REVEREND M. J. NOL N. PASTOR · WILLIAM F. CODY. A.I.A.. ARCHITECT

Considered alongside the executed project, this preliminary, angular scheme shows Cody's facility with a diversity of architectural elements and materials.

in the Church … to contribute its own voice to that wonderful chorus of praise in honor of the Catholic faith sung by great men in times gone by." This recognition of contemporary art must have resonated with Cody's belief in modern art and architecture, and the designs he produced for the altars and baptismal font represent modern visions of Catholic furnishings. Cody surely also supported the belief that the art of the Church "should strive after noble beauty rather than mere sumptuous display." While most of Cody's other projects relied on the straight line (and a rendering for an earlier design for St. Theresa shows a much more rectilinear scheme), the final design for this church uses dynamic, elegant curves throughout, as seen in the graceful altars and ovoid baptismal font, in the upward sweep of the crossing, and in the profiles of the wooden beams. As in so many historical Catholic churches, in St. Theresa the eye is drawn upward by light, here streaming from the skylight over the high altar where the priest celebrates the sacrament of the Holy Eucharist. Above the skylight, the spire comprises four curved, steel-and-wood elements joined at the top, a composition that suggests hands held together in prayer. Cody also designed the Celtic cross that crowns the building. All in all, Cody's innovative,

elegant design for St. Theresa's amply demonstrates the "noble beauty" called for by the Vatican Council.

In addition, the church is a masterwork of total design for which Cody relied on highly skilled artists and artisans to realize his vision. Cody himself designed the altars, pews, baptismal font, and sanctuary furniture. Finding no one in the United States willing to attempt the simple but very delicate travertine altars, Cody turned to Sicea Marmi of Lucca, Italy. He commissioned Doezie Custom Furniture of Santa Fe Springs, California, to construct the wooden furnishings, notably the pews of Australian walnut. Barnabas Wasson, a sculptor from Yarnell, Arizona, designed the tabernacle of the altar of the Blessed Sacrament, the Cross of the Resurrection above the tabernacle, the Stations of the Cross, and other furnishings.

In 1979, the year after Cody's death, St. Theresa Church received the Golden Palm Award for architectural excellence, a fitting coda to Cody's remarkable career.

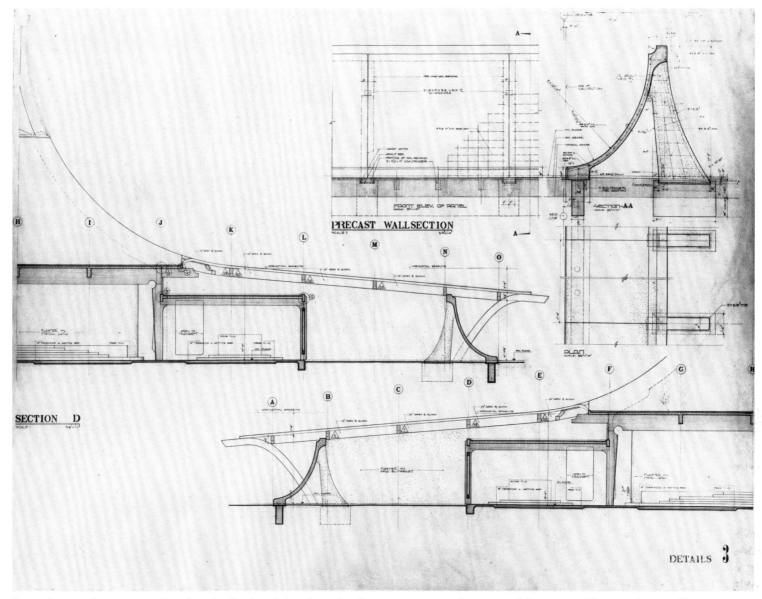

Section drawings showing curves throughout the church, including the roof profile, precast concrete wall sections, and the junction of the nave columns and beams.

The baptistry lies between the nave and vestibule, its circular shape linking it to a long history of centralized baptistries. The shape of the baptismal font refers to the egg as a symbol of Christian resurrection.

View across the nave to the west chapel. The opening in the right side of the chapel wall allows views of the sanctuary from the chapel.

The four surfaces of the ceiling rise above the sanctuary to frame a skylight.

A curved plaster wall serves as the backdrop for the sanctuary. Jos Maes designed the stained glass to the sides and Barnabas Wasson created the crucifix, tabernacle, and tiered candelabras (shown used as planters).

The southeast corner of the church enclosure, showing the poured-in-place concrete wall.

Vertical wooden fins on the entrance door partition the stained glass panels by Jos Maes.

Altar of the Celebration of the Eucharist, with view of the nave toward the baptistry and vestibule.

Wall buttresses in the east meditation garden.

A circular cutout adorns the connection between the glulam beams and columns.

February 20, 1966, groundbreaking ceremony for the church. Cody is wielding the shovel, and Reverend Michael J. Nolan stands to his left. Bishop Furey of San Diego is second from right, and Father Thomas Flahive, pastor of Our Lady of Guadalupe church, is at right.

# McCulloch Plaza/ McCulloch Oil Corporation Headquarters

Los Angeles | California | 1969 (unbuilt)

Beginning with Eldorado Country Club, Robert P. McCulloch was one of Cody's most prolific and adventurous clients, providing the architect with opportunities to design not only individual buildings but also large-scale master plans. As an inventor and entrepreneur, McCulloch was perhaps best known for McCulloch Corporation and its namesake chain saws, for which Cody designed a proposed main plant (unbuilt) in Lake Havasu City in 1967; the project included a 275,000-square-foot plant plus more than 167,000 square feet of other industrial, office, and research space. In addition to McCulloch Corporation, McCulloch established McCulloch Oil, McCulloch Aircraft Corporation, and Paxton Automotive, among others. In 1968, he famously bought London Bridge, which he reassembled in Lake Havasu City—one of several cities he founded—to attract visitors and potential residents.

In 1970, McCulloch asked Cody to design the headquarters for McCulloch Oil, to be located just a few blocks northeast of Los Angeles International Airport. The proposal for this commercial project, one

of the largest of Cody's career, included office blocks ranging from seven to ten stories high. Like his library design for CSU San Bernardino, the plans for these McCulloch buildings use concrete in several textures and colors. The overall composition of the complex is asymmetric and dynamic, but Cody's application of a regular, repeated window module unifies the various parts. Unfortunately, this project was never executed.

Opposite and above, two views of model of McCulloch Plaza in Los Angeles, planned to house McCulloch Oil Corporation Headquarters, Computer Center, and Airport-Marina Industrial Center.

# California State University, San Bernardino Library, Audio-Visual and Classroom Building

San Bernardino │ California │ 1971

At the heart of the Cal State San Bernardino campus stands the John M. Pfau Library, a five-story concrete building designed by Cody in association with the Claremont firm of Criley & McDowell. In 1966, the architects worked with the building committee, librarian Arthur E. Nelson, and executive dean Dr. Joseph K. Thomas to develop the program for this 110,000-square-foot building for California State College at San Bernardino, as the campus was then called. Construction began in August 1968 and was completed in 1971 after a year of delays caused by bad weather. Containing the library, classrooms, and other facilities, and originally simply called the College Library, it was renamed the John M. Pfau Library in 1982 to honor the university's first president. A new wing was added in 1994.

From the south, the primary entry, visitors see the library against the backdrop of the Shandin Hills as they approach up a broad set of shallow stairs to the library terrace. Although abstract and geometric like many institutional buildings of the era, the CSUSB Library suggests classical architecture in its symmetry, clarity, and regular openings. As in many of his other designs, including the Palm Springs Spa Hotel and Eldorado Country Club, Cody maximized the expressive potential of concrete. For example, the "grille" that marks the main facades on the north and south is composed of light-colored precast elements, while sand-colored, vertically striated concrete is used for the building's corners. The elevated wings on the east and west are covered with a different textured concrete on the long sides and precast frames on the ends. Because the building sits within a half mile of the San Andreas Fault, great attention was given to the reinforced-concrete structure.

The CSUSB Library is a reminder that Cody was devoted not so much to a particular style as to a set of approaches that focused on setting, client, and materials. His residential designs, for instance those along the Eldorado Country Club fairways, were closely integrated with their desert and country club environments and planned to accommodate the preferred lifestyles of their owners. The result was often openness and asymmetry. In contrast, the CSUSB Library was solid and symmetric, the product of the desire to create a monumental center for the campus and to house books and classrooms.

Presentation drawing showing view from the southeast.

Grooves in the ceiling echo the shape of the door's horizontal glass inserts, while lights in the ceiling inside mirror the form of the door's circular inserts.

Cody exploited concrete in many ways for a variety of uses, including paving, benches, and several different brise-soleil systems.

Notches in the floor plate and between the paired windows continue the vertical line of the columns.

View of the main entrance from the southwest.

Close-up of brise-soleil system used on the front and back of the building, showing the details of the precast concrete components.

# Samuel and Gladys Rubinstein Residence

Rancho Mirage | California | 1972

After Samuel and Gladys Rubinstein bought a fairway lot at the Tamarisk Country Club for their winter residence, a neighbor directed them to Bill Cody. Gladys brought cutouts of Mexican homes and gardens for Cody to consider, and the Rubinsteins then returned to their summer home in Seattle. After discussing the initial proposal, which did not match Gladys's vision, Cody produced another design the following year; Gladys deemed this one more "magnificent" even than what she had imagined. What made the architecture of the Rubinstein Residence so distinctive was Cody's synthesis of his modernism with the Rubinsteins' preferred hacienda-style architecture.

From the street, the house presents a long, simple stucco wall with a low-pitched tile roof, reminiscent of haciendas in Mexico or Mission-style homes in California. Upon entry, visitors find themselves in a spacious courtyard with electrically operated overhead glass panels that can be closed during inclement weather. Designed for entertaining, the living spaces are generous and open; for instance, the living room is connected to the courtyard on one side and the covered patio on the other, allowing easy circulation from inside to outside. The billiard room, which contains a sunken bar, also opens to the courtyard. This spatial fluidity, as well as the lack of architectural ornament, is a basic characteristic of Cody's modernist residential designs.

However, in contrast with the spatial planning, the palette of materials is more typical of Mission-style architecture: red quarry tile throughout the living spaces, exposed wooden beams, and thick, textured stucco walls. Here, as in the Monterey model house he had designed for Desert Bel Air Estates, Cody eschewed the lightness of his steel-framed designs, such as the Shamel Residence, for the solidity typical of Mission-style buildings. One advantage is environmental: even more than most of Cody's houses, the Rubinstein Residence is well-adapted to the extreme heat and light of the desert. None of the major living spaces have openings to the east or west, and all are protected from the sun by deep roof overhangs or porches to the south. The high, sloping ceilings allow hot air to rise, making the rooms more comfortable in warmer weather.

The Rubinsteins collected contemporary and indigenous art and displayed it throughout the house. For example, the dining room displayed a row of platters by Pablo Picasso on one wall, an Italo Scanga painting on another, and a large blown-glass centerpiece by Dale Chihuly on the dining table—one of several Chihuly works in the house. The renowned artist Claire Falkenstein created the dramatic metal and colored-glass entry doors as well as a wall sculpture by the swimming pool and a tabletop sculpture in the living room. A large painting

A Viola Frey sculpture reclines by the swimming pool.

The tile roofs and stucco walls visible from the street suggest the hacienda-style buildings admired by Gladys Rubinstein.

by Roberto Matta hung over the living room fireplace. Cody designed niches of floating shelves around the house to show off smaller objects; each shelf is set off from the wall behind, the recessed lighting in its back edge illuminating the niche and its artworks. For the interiors, Gladys hired the San Francisco interior designer Barry Brukoff, who worked with Cody's design and with the Rubinsteins' art collection. Brukoff later stated that he enjoyed working with Cody and they discussed the possibility of future projects, but were unable to do so before Cody suffered a stroke in 1973.

The Rubinsteins' appreciation of Cody and his design for their home is evidenced by the forty-two years they occupied the house without making any changes. After Cody's stroke, they invited him to their home once a month when they were in residence, and Gladys referred to him as "my architect."

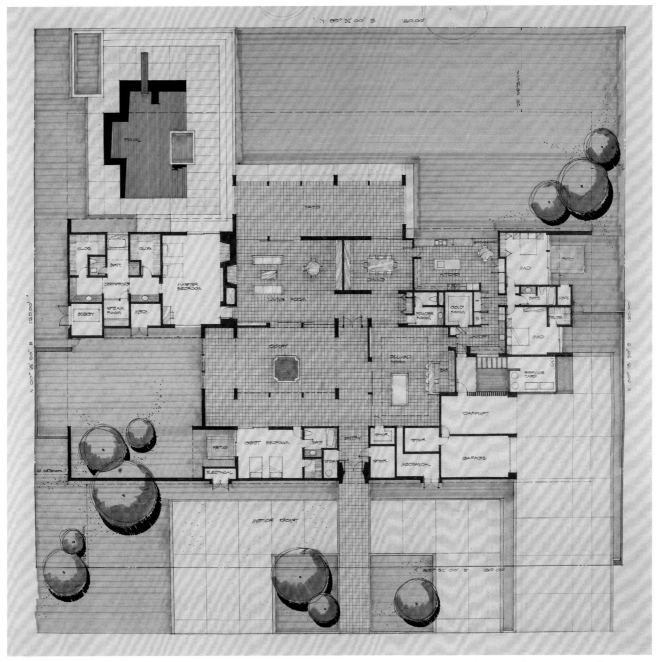

Designed for entertaining and art, the Rubinstein Residence borders the Tamarisk Country Club fairway to the south. The courtyard pond was not built.

The gates in the opaque entry facade open to a courtyard from which the guest room, billiard room, and main living spaces are accessible. Cody designed the wall lantern as a housewarming gift for the Rubinsteins.

The entry courtyard with Cody's favored wood ceilings and quarry tile. The door to the guest quarters lies beyond the sculpture next to the left wall.

Once inside the outer gate, the visitor passes through the entry courtyard to custom interior doors by Claire Falkenstein. The living room, connected to the courtyard for optimal entertaining, is visible to the left.

Seen from the foyer, the small openings and colored glass of the Claire Falkenstein doors suggest stained glass windows.

View off the living room with custom, backlighted display shelving.

The billiard room includes a sunken bar and a custom billiard table by Barry Brukoff.

In the dining room, the Rubensteins displayed a set of ceramic platters by Pablo Picasso and a painting by Italo Scanga.
Barry Brukoff designed the walnut-and-teak veneered dining table and buffet.

In the kitchen, Cody created continuous surfaces of wood veneer. The cobalt blue tile from Heath Ceramics also appears in the primary bathroom.

The expansive patio on the south side of the living room and dining room offers fairway views and shaded space for entertaining.

# Andreas Hills and Whitewater Country Club

Palm Springs | California | 1972–75

Harry F. Chaddick, who had worked extensively with Cody at the Palm Springs Tennis Club, also commissioned him for two other major projects: Andreas Hills and Whitewater Country Club. In 1968, Chaddick announced the former, a development of condominiums, single-family homes, and a luxury hotel (not executed) on a 643-acre site in south Palm Springs. He hired Cody for the master plan of this new subdivision, which he claimed would become the "Bel Air" of Palm Springs, referring to the exclusive residential community in Los Angeles. In addition to the master plan, Cody designed the condos for the second and third phases of Andreas Hills, receiving an Award of Excellence from the Inland California Chapter of the AIA for his phase 2 work. (The twenty condos of the first phase of Andreas Hills were designed by Ed Walker.) Each of the three condo complexes was organized around a generous green space with a swimming pool; buyers of homes in Andreas Hills were given free membership in either the Palm Springs Tennis Club or the Whitewater Country Club, part of Chaddick's desire to sell a complete vision of the Palm Springs lifestyle.

In 1969, Chaddick purchased San Jacinto Country Club and renamed it Whitewater Country Club (later changing the name to Palm Springs Country Club in 1976 to avoid confusion with an unrelated community northeast of Palm Springs). He immediately embarked on extensive renovations and additions to turn it into a complete leisure community with tennis courts, swimming pool, and other facilities in addition to an improved golf course. He hired Cody to design the master plan, 236 condominium units, and the clubhouse, which was dedicated on November 25, 1972. For the condos, Cody conceived four types of buildings containing a total of six different unit plans, ranging in size from one bedroom/885 square feet to three bedrooms/1,430 square feet. In Cody's master plan, each condo building is placed next to a different type of condo building, ensuring variety throughout the complex. As at Andreas Hills, the condos were grouped around green spaces with swimming pools. Ground was broken for the condos in September 1971, and the sixty units in phase 1 were completed in spring 1972; the thirty-eight phase 2 units were finished in January 1975. Cody's stroke prevented him from designing the condos for phases 3 and 4, which were handled instead by Bernard Leung.

Recreation area of the phase 2 condominiums seen from the northwest.

Phase 2 condominiums are in the left half of the highlighted area, phase 3 in the right. Google Earth, Image 2019 Landsat / Copernicus.

Phase 2 condominiums seen from the east; the original open-air carports were later converted to garages.

Phase 2 condominiums seen from the west.

Phase 3 condominiums seen from the east.

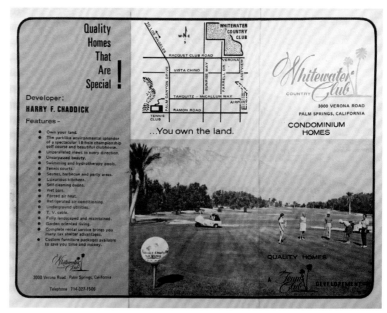

Considered alongside projects such as Mission Valley Country Club and Eldorado Country Club, the solidity and thick stucco walls of Whitewater Country Club show the remarkable range of Cody's golf club architecture.

As at the Palm Springs Tennis Club, Chaddick and Cody envisioned a comprehensive, modern resort community.

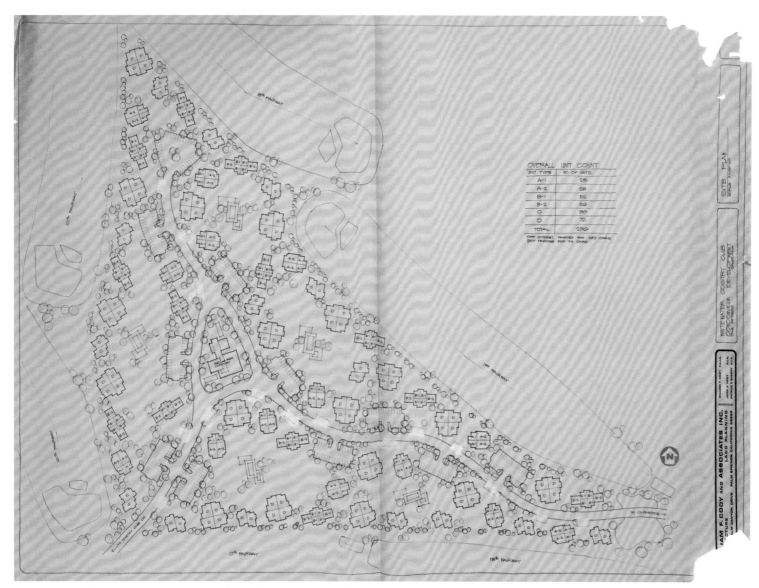

Fairways surround the 236 condominium units of the Whitewater Country Club residential area.

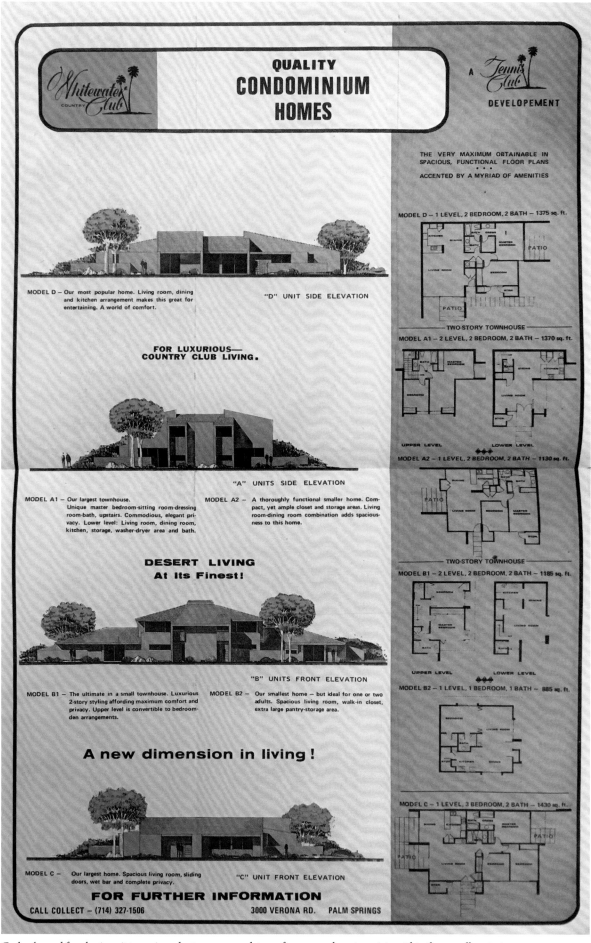

Cody planned four basic unit types in order to accommodate preferences and create variety within the overall project.

# Palm Springs Public Library

Palm Springs | California | 1975

While serving as the city architect for Palm Springs, Cody headed the Palm Springs Collaborative, a group of local architects that proposed a set of recreational facilities to be called Highland Community Park. At the time, the Welwood Murray Memorial Library, which had opened in 1941, was the city's main library, but at only 4,030 square feet it was far too small for a city whose population had grown sixfold since 1940. Cody's new 30,000-square-foot library, the only one of the proposed buildings to be constructed, was designed to house 150,000 volumes.

Like St. Theresa Church nearby, the library is an inward-oriented building surrounded by sloping walls, appearing as a kind of protected sanctuary. The thick walls and overhanging roof buffer the light and heat of Palm Springs, with clerestory windows admitting views to the sky while protecting sensitive materials from direct sunlight. A central skylight and pond enhance the serenity of the interior. Completed in 1975, this building remains the main library in Palm Springs.

December 7, 1975, library dedication. Front row from left: Bert Wills and Bill Cody; back row from left: Francis Crocker, Mary Fahr, Elizabeth Coffman Kieley, Marge Crommelin, city librarian Billie Lu Floan, councilman Elliot Field, councilman Russ Beirich, Bob Schlesinger, Don Blubaugh, Mayor Bill Foster, and councilman Joe Garcia. Foster was also the contractor for St. Theresa's Church and other Cody projects.

David Purciel rendering of the library's original main entrance on the south side.

View of the current entrance on the east side of the library.

View from the southeast, showing the battered exterior concrete walls.

Model of the library showing the placement of the building at an angle to the street grid.

Sculpture by Philip Culbertson on the east side court, later to become the front entrance.

Postcard showing the skylights over the central water feature, with the circulation desk in the background.

# William F. Cody Projects

Rendering for an addition to The Desert Inn, 1945, Palm Springs.

*The projects compiled here have been drawn from various archival sources including contracts, correspondence, presentation and internal working drawings, and construction documents. Years assigned may be of project completion years, design dates, or dates otherwise appearing in their source documents. There remain dozens of projects not listed here that lack information regarding location, date, or status of completion, but for which references can be found in the Special Collections and Archives at the Kennedy Library, California Polytechnic State University, San Luis Obispo.*

### 1943

- Brian Aherne and Joan Fontaine Residence (for Cliff May), Indio, California
- Open Hearth Steel Plant, design and drawings, for Donald R. Warren Company, Fontana, California
- Installations for Treasure Island Naval Base and outlying facilities, design and drawings (for Blanchard, Maher and Ward Architects), San Francisco, California

### 1944–46

- Corona del Mar Elementary School, Corona del Mar, California; Suva Elementary School, Bell Gardens, California; Coachella Valley Union School, Thermal, California; Coachella Valley Baptist Church, Thermal, California; Montebello High School Music Building, California; Claremont High School, Claremont, California; Big Bear High School, Big Bear, California; Bell Gardens High School, Bell Gardens, California; Laguna Beach Unified School District Building, Laguna Beach, California; University of Redlands Life Sciences Building, Redlands, California; UCLA Administration and Maintenance Building, Los Angeles, California (as lead designer, March, Smith and Powell)

### 1944

- Pace-Setter House (with Cliff May), Los Angeles, California

### 1945

- Blue Haven restaurant and nightclub, Long Beach, California

### 1946

- Castellammare Market, Pacific Palisades, California
- Day Residence (alteration), West Los Angeles, California
- Desert Center Motel, Desert Center, California
- The Desert Inn (alteration and addition, for Nellie N. Coffman), Palm Springs, California
- Desert Palms Estates Swimming Club (for Paul Belding), Palm Springs, California (unbuilt)
- Dorresten Residence, Smoke Tree Ranch, Palm Springs, California
- Gene Dursch Residence, Malibu, California
- Flagstaff housing, multi-residential, Flagstaff, Arizona
- Hotel (for Louise Kerr and family), Westwood Village, Los Angeles, California
- Roy King Residence (alteration), West Los Angeles, California
- Annie Plymire and Jennie Lawson Residence, Palm Springs, California
- South Winds Motel (for Gene Dursch), Malibu, California
- Woodley Apartments, Santa Monica, California

Proposed design drawing for the Desert Palms Estates Swimming Club, a community recreational and social club, 1946, Palm Springs (unbuilt).

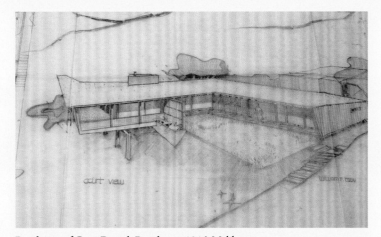

Rendering of Gene Dursch Residence, 1946, Malibu.

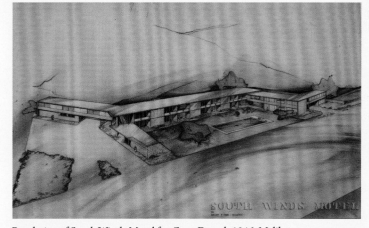

Rendering of South Winds Motel for Gene Dursch,1946, Malibu.

Rendering Louise Kerr and family hotel, 1946, Westwood Village, Los Angeles.

Rendering of Woodley Apartments, 1945, Santa Monica.

Renderings for Village Church of the West in association with local architect Ralph B. Haver, 1948, Phoenix, Arizona (unbuilt). Mercer Mortuary Chapel (1950, Phoenix) would use a similar design.

## 1947

- Charles and Winifred Becker Residence (alteration), Palm Springs, California
- Paul and Anita Belding Residence, Desert Palms Estates, Palm Springs, California
- Frank M. Bogert and Janice L. Bibo Residence, Thunderbird Ranch, Rancho Mirage, California
- Del Marcos Apartment Hotel, Palm Springs, California
- Dominic de Rosa ( alteration and addition), Palm Springs, California
- Flagstaff Elementary School and Dunbar Elementary School with Gilmore and Varney Architects, Flagstaff, Arizona
- Flagstaff High School and Gymnasium with Gilmore and Varney Architects, Flagstaff, Arizona
- Flagstaff Orpheum Theatre (for Paramount–Nace Theatres), Flagstaff, Arizona
- Russell D. Garner Residence, Palm Desert, California
- Display House #1 and 2 (for Grace Realty), Las Palmas Estates, Palm Springs, California
- Ferde Grofé Residence, Santa Monica, California
- Henderson Building, office/apartment units (for Carl Henderson), Palm Desert, California (no longer extant)
- Hubbell Residence (alteration), Palm Springs, California
- La Vista Grande Guest Lodge (for Paul Feltman), Rancho Marizona, Phoenix, Arizona
- Mike Levee, Jr. Residence, Thunderbird Ranch, Rancho Mirage, California
- Dorothy Levin Residence, Desert Palms Estates, Palm Springs, California
- Mandel Residence (alteration), Palm Springs, California
- May Residence (alteration), Palm Springs, California
- Nuevo Apartment Hotel, Phoenix, Arizona
- Palo Verde Primary School (for Marsh, Smith and Powell), Blythe, California
- Spurgin Office Building, Malibu, California
- Wentworth Residence, Sedona, Arizona

## 1948

- Dr. Carlson Bates Residence, Bridgeport, Arizona
- Bud Domke Apartments, Palm Springs, California
- El Capri Apartment Hotel (addition), Palm Springs, California
- Charles H. and Jean Feltman Residence, Playa del Rey, California
- Fishman Store and Apartment Building, Palm Springs, California
- E. F. Gates Medical Building, Santa Monica, California
- Hotel del Tahquitz (addition), Palm Springs, California
- Kier Residence (alteration), Los Angeles, California
- Lo Sasso Units, Santa Monica, California
- Hutch and Billy Mosley Residence, Palm Springs, California
- James Pelican Residence, West Los Angeles, California
- Three residences for Richard Rand Construction Company, Palm Springs, California
- Lot 7 residence (with Stefan S. Ryciak), Rancho Marizona, Phoenix, Arizona
- Sedona Elementary School, Sedona, Arizona
- Village Church of the West (with Ralph B. Haver), 1948, Phoenix, Arizona, (unbuilt)
- Worcester Hotel, Palm Springs, California
- George Wright Residence, Thunderbird Ranch, Rancho Mirage, California

## 1949

- Cahill office and manufacturing facility, Beverly Hills, California
- Spec. House #1 and 2 (for Fidler-Zagon Investment Corp.), Desert Palms Estates, Palm Springs, California
- Flagstaff Airport Administration Building (with Edward L. Varney), Flagstaff, Arizona
- Flagstaff City Hall (with Edward L. Varney), Flagstaff, Arizona
- Haines studio and offices (for William Haines), Beverly Hills, California
- Barney Hinkle Residence, Thunderbird Ranch, Rancho Mirage, California
- Laguta Hotel, Palm Springs, California
- Manners Motel, Palm Springs, California
- Module and Sand Star Houses, Hidden Springs, California
- Our Lady of Malibu Catholic Church, Malibu, California
- Palm Springs Tramway Mountain Terminal Proposal (for Mount San Jacinto Winter Park Authority), Palm Springs, California (unbuilt)

Rendering of the winning design for the Flagstaff High School and Gymnasium, 1946, Flagstaff, Arizona.

Rendering of Orpheum Theatre for Paramount-Nace Theatres, 1947, Flagstaff.

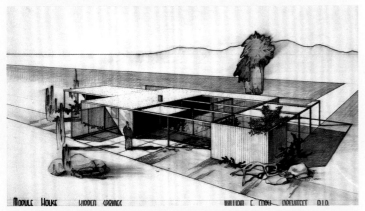

Rendering of the Module House, 1949, Hidden Springs.

Rendering of Dr. Robert A. Franklyn Residence, 1949, Los Angeles.

Agua Caliente Resort Hotel and Spa, c. 1950, Palm Springs (unbuilt). Similar to Cody's designs for the Villa Real Country Club Hotel in Havana and for the Cameron Shopping Center in Palm Springs, Cody juxtaposes long horizontal angled planes to create dynamic compositions (delineated by Shrewsbury – Nichols).

Paul and Anita Belding Residence, 1947, Palm Springs (delineated by John R. Hollingsworth).

Rendering of the Sand Star House, 1949, Hidden Springs.

Rendering of Airport Administration Building, 1949, Flagstaff, Arizona from Cody's projects portfolio, 1958.

Cody's sense of humor is revealed in his rendering for Mercer Funeral Home with a skull rock and artery landscaping in the foreground, 1950, Phoenix, Arizona.

- Grace K. Randall Residence, Phoenix, Arizona
- Dr. Robert A. Franklyn Residence, Los Angeles, California

### 1950
- Agua Caliente Resort Hotel and Spa, Palm Springs, 1948 design year, California (unbuilt)
- Carl H. Anderson Residence, Thunderbird Country Club, Rancho Mirage, California
- John Dawson Residence, Thunderbird Country Club, Rancho Mirage, California
- El Portel Hotel (addition, for Herman N. Fink, Laguta Realty), Palm Springs, California
- Major Reuben and Eva May Fleet Residence, Palm Springs, California
- Frederic J. Grant Residence, Smoke Tree Ranch, Palm Springs, California
- Harthern Residence, Los Angeles, California
- Pro Larson Residence (alteration), Santa Monica, California
- Lippitt Car Wash (remodel), San Diego, California
- D.B. McDaniel Residence, Thunderbird Country Club, Rancho Mirage, California
- Milbank McFie Residence, Smoke Tree Ranch, Palm Springs, California
- Dr. J. P. McNally Residence, Prescott, Arizona
- Mercer Funeral Home and Chapel (with Fred Weaver), Phoenix, Arizona
- Palm Springs City Park north end, Palm Springs, California
- Thunderbird Country Club Estates Tract Map Development, Rancho Mirage, California
- Thunderbird Country Club master plan and clubhouse (alteration and addition, for John Dawson), Rancho Mirage, California
- Thunderbird Shopping Center (for John Dawson), Rancho Mirage, California (unbuilt)
- Waffle Shop (alteration), Palm Springs, California
- Sam and Mary Zimbalist Residence, Malibu, California

### 1951
- Guy Anderson Residence (alteration), Palm Springs, California
- Stores & Offices for M. H. Atikian, Palm Springs, California
- Broken Arrow Hotel, Palm Springs, California

- George E. Jr. and Daphne Cameron Residence, Thunderbird Country Club, Rancho Mirage, California
- Christmas Tree Plaza Hotel, Apartments, and Shopping Center, Flagstaff, Arizona
- Walt and Lily Disney Residence, Smoke Tree Ranch, Palm Springs, California
- Paul V. Feltman Residence, Rancho Marizona, Phoenix, Arizona
- Roland Feltman Residence (with Ralf Haver), Arizona
- Kraftex Enterprises Inc. office building, Houston, Texas
- Multiresidential project (for La Jolla Development Company), La Jolla, California
- La Paz Hotel, Cody-McWethy Development, Palm Springs, California
- Paris Letsinger Residence, Thunderbird Country Club, Rancho Mirage, California
- Cliff May Residence, Palm Springs, California
- McManus Drive-In Theater, Palm Springs, California
- Orchid Tree Inn Hotel (alteration and addition), Palm Springs, California
- Dr. Hough Phillips Residence, Cottage #8 (alteration), Thunderbird Country Club, Rancho Mirage, California
- Sea Level Corporation Building, Palm Springs, California
- George W. Scrimshaw Residence, Thunderbird Country Club, Rancho Mirage, California
- Walter Smyth Residence, Palm Springs, California
- Sun Air Flame Unit and Firebird Lodge, Cody-McWethy Development, Cathedral City, California
- Thunderbird Valley Estates, Warburton Properties Development, Rancho Mirage, California

### 1952
- M. O. Anderson Residence, Tamarisk Country Club, Rancho Mirage, California
- William and Winifred Cody Residence, Desert Palms Estates, Palm Springs, California
- H. H. Foster Residence, Palm Springs, California
- Milton Hicks Car Agency (alteration), Palm Springs, California
- L'Horizon Hotel (for Jack Wrather and Bonita Granville), Palm Springs, California

Carl Anderson & Residence, 1950, Rancho Mirage.

Our Lady of Malibu Catholic Church, 1949, Malibu.

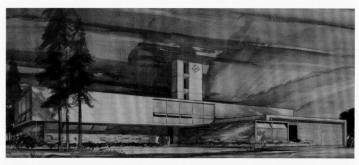

Rendering of Flagstaff City Hall, designed in association with architect Edward L. Varney, 1949, Flagstaff, Arizona.

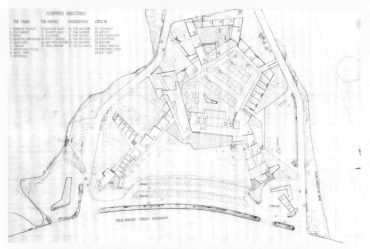

Master plan drawing for Thunderbird Shopping Center, July 1950, Rancho Mirage, (unbuilt).

Cody's drawings for a pavilion and park with water features, Arizona.

Rendering of Walt and Lily Disney Residence, 1951, Palm Springs.

Flame Unit, 1951, Cathedral City.

Rendering of George and Daphne Cameron Residence, 1951, Rancho Mirage.

- Joseph J. and Bernice A. Malone Residence, Desert Palms Estates, Palm Springs, California
- McManus Center Development building (for Pearl McManus), Palm Springs, California
- McManus Hotel apartments, Palm Springs, California
- Edward Miller Residence, Thunderbird Country Club, Rancho Mirage, California
- Palm Springs Airport shop building, Palm Springs, California
- Palm Springs Turf Club (with Wayne McAllister and William C. Wagner), Palm Springs, California (unbuilt)
- William Perlberg and Bobbe Brox Residence, Palm Springs, California
- Snow Summit Mountain Resort, Big Bear, California

### 1953
- Irving & Alma Babroff Residence, Deepwell Estates, Palm Springs, California
- Desert Club (addition), Borrego Springs, California
- Joe G. Dyer Residence, Thunderbird Country Club, Rancho Mirage, California
- Jockey Club of Las Vegas, Las Vegas, Nevada
- Kenneth B. Kirk office building, Dallas, Texas
- La Jollan Hotel (with Paul R. Williams), La Jolla, California
- Maddick, Mead Desert Club tract, La Quinta, California
- Palm Springs Tahquitz Company Development, Palm Springs, California
- Austin H. Peterson Residence, (purchased new by Frank Sinatra) Wonder Palms Estates, Rancho Mirage, California
- Tamarisk Country Club clubhouse (with Martin Stern Jr.), Rancho Mirage, California
- Westlake Builders Company, Rancho Mirage, California

### 1954
- Allen Avery Residence, Tamarisk Country Club, Rancho Mirage, California
- Waldo Avery Residence, Rancho Mirage, California
- Irv Berman office building, Beverly Hills, California
- Blue Skies Trailer Village, Master Plan, and Clubhouse (for Bing Crosby), Rancho Mirage, California

- William T. Byrne Residence, Deepwell Estates, Palm Springs, California
- Arthur Cary Residence, Palm Springs, California
- Chaddwicks Restaurant (addition), San Diego, California
- Gerstenzang and Busse Residence, Palm Springs, California
- Googie's Restaurant (for Ed Thurston), Beverly Hills, California
- Frank R. and Dorothy Long Residence, Beverly Hills, California
- Manseau Hotel Units, Thunderbird Country Club, Rancho Mirage, California
- Lou and Ruth Manseau Residence (on Manseau Hotel property), Rancho Mirage, California
- John McCallum Residence (relocation), Palm Springs, California
- Mission Valley Golf Club and Hotel, San Diego, California
- Mottells Mortuary (for Don Peek), Long Beach, California
- L.L. Oakes Residence, Thunderbird Country Club, Rancho Mirage, California
- Rief Residence, San Diego, California
- Frank Ruben Residence, Palm Desert, California
- Sunset Tower shops, apartments, and offices, Palm Springs, California
- Thunderbird Park subdivision, Indio, California

### 1955
- Araby Point Estates, Palm Springs, California
- Frank Belcher Residence, Thunderbird Country Club, Rancho Mirage, California
- Hoagy Carmichael Residence (addition), Thunderbird Country Club, Rancho Mirage, California
- Ray and Dorothy Blumenthal Residence, Deepwell Estates, Palm Springs, California
- Desert Estates development (for Mottle and Jones), Palm Springs, California
- Edificio Mateal apartment and office building (for María Teresa and Alvaro González Gordon), Havana, Cuba (unbuilt)
- Ted Freistat Residence, Los Angeles, California
- Ted Freistat Restaurant, Los Angeles, California
- Earle M. Jorgensen Residence, Thunderbird Country Club, Rancho Mirage, California
- Milton and Zephyr Karahadian Residence, Tamarisk Country Club, Rancho Mirage, California

East elevation of Stores & Offices for M. H. Atikian on Palm Canyon Drive, 1951, Palm Springs.

Proposed Palm Springs Turf Club by Wayne McAllister, & Wm. C. Wagner, Wm. F. Cody, AIA, Architects, 1952, Palm Springs (unbuilt).

Tamarisk Country Club Clubhouse (with Martin Stern, Jr.), 1953, Rancho Mirage (rendering by Gene Shrewsbury).

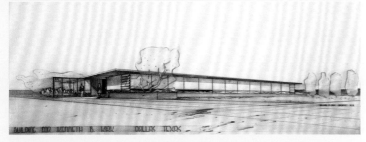

Cody rendering for Kenneth B. Kirk Office Building, 1953, Dallas, Texas.

Joseph J. And Bernice A. Malone Residence, 1952, Palm Springs.

William Perlberg and Bobbe Brox Residence, 1952, Palm Springs. Cantilevered angled mailbox identifies the home address. Inside, glass walls meet perpendicularly at a corner post, expanding the outdoor views and the roof protected outdoor dining patio.

Arthur Cary Residence, 1954, Palm Springs.

Blue Skies Trailer Village Master Plan, Clubhouse & Service Buildings for Bing Crosby. Regarded as the "first of the high-end trailer parks.,"
1954, Rancho Mirage (rendering by Gene Shrewsbury).

Cody rendering for Frank Ruben Residence, 1954, Palm Desert.

Sunset Tower Building, 1954, Palm Springs.

Waldo Avery Residence, 1954, Rancho Mirage.

Silverado Country Club, 1955, Napa (delineated by Shrewsbury – Nichols).

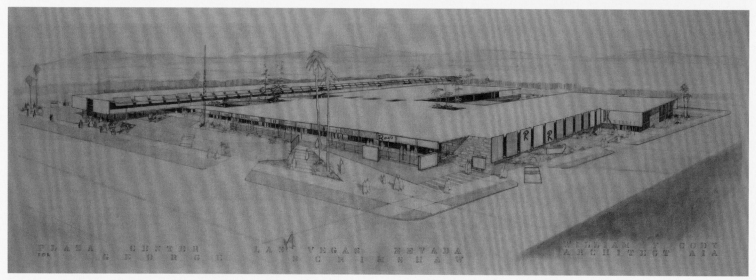

Rendering of Las Vegas Plaza Center, 1955, Las Vegas, Nevada.

W.A. Moncrief Residence, 1955, Rancho Mirage.

A. Pollard Simons Residence, 1956, Rancho Mirage.

David C. Holub Residence, 1956, Rancho Mirage.

Rendering of Gleason Point Development Resort Apartments, 1956, San Diego.

John Gillin Residence, 1957, Rancho Mirage.

Rendering of residence at Tamarisk Country Club for Jimmy Hines, 1956, Rancho Mirage.

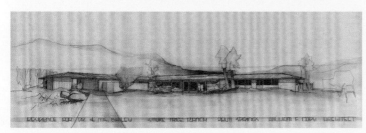

Rendering for Dr. Wilbur Bailey Residence, 1957, Palm Springs.

Recreation Area, Marin Hotel Sports Club for Paul Trousdale and Associates, 1957, San Rafael (rendering by J. R. Hollingsworth, unbuilt).

Cameron Center east elevation with Cody annex office at the right end, 1958–61, Palm Springs.

- Jack Meiselman Residence, Desert Palms Estates, Palm Springs, California
- Meiselman & Rosenbaum Residence, Palm Springs, California
- Model Home (for Mottle and Jones), Desert Estates development, Palm Springs, California
- Carl Mueller Residence (with Henry Hester), San Diego, California
- Peckham Residence (with Henry Hester), San Diego, California
- Plaza Center (for George Scrimshaw), Las Vegas, Nevada
- Silverado Golf Country Club clubhouse and cottages (alteration, for John W. Dawson Co.), Napa, California
- Tahquitz River Estates development, Palm Springs, California
- Dr. Taylor Residence (with Henry Hester), San Diego, California
- Thunderbird Country Club – 4th Fairway guest cottages, Rancho Mirage, California
- Valle Alto Country Club clubhouse and hotel (with Lawrence Hughes, golf course architect, for Jaime M. Gutierrez), Monterrey, Mexico
- Villa Real Golf Country Club (master plan, clubhouse, and hotel, for María Teresa and Alvaro González Gordon), Havana, Cuba (unbuilt)
- Westover Residence, 1955, West Los Angeles, California

**1956**
- George Cameron Jr. Office alteration, Palm Springs, California
- Cameron Radio Transmitter Station (KDES, for George Cameron Jr.), Palm Springs, California
- Desert Car Wash (for Ray Corliss), Palm Springs, California
- Sherwood Egbert Residence, Thunderbird Country Club, Rancho Mirage, California
- Ellsworth Automobile Agency, Palm Springs, California
- Ewald Residence, Thunderbird Country Club, Rancho Mirage, California
- Gleason Point Development resort apartments, San Diego, California
- James (Jimmy) Hines Residence, Thunderbird North, Rancho Mirage, California
- David C. Holub Residence, Tamarisk Country Club, Rancho Mirage, California
- Lynn Jennings Residence (alteration), Palm Springs, California
- J. E. Kistan Country Club, Houston, Texas
- Eugenio Garza Lagüera Residence (alteration), Monterrey, Mexico
- La Quinta Hotel and Cottages (alteration and addition), La Quinta, California
- A. Pollard Simons Residence, Thunderbird North, Rancho Mirage, California
- W. A. Moncrief Residence, Thunderbird North, Rancho Mirage, California

- Charles W. Moran Residence, San Diego, California
- Pearson Shopping Center, San Bernardino, California
- Planta Principal (for Eugenio Garza Lagüera), Monterrey, Mexico
- Tropicana Gardens Development (for Fillmore Crank), Las Vegas, Nevada
- Martin Pollard Residence, Rancho Mirage, California
- Saddle and Sirloin Restaurant (addition), Palm Springs, California
- Silberman Residence (with Henry Hester), San Diego, California
- The Springs Restaurant (for George Cameron, Jr.), Cameron Center, Palm Springs, California (no longer extant)
- R. I. Thorsdale Residence (alteration), Palm Springs, California

**1957**
- Dr. Wilbur and Margaret Bailey Residence, Smoke Tree Ranch, Palm Springs, California
- Bethlehem Steel Corporation (addition), South San Francisco, California
- Housing for California Development Company (with Henry Hester), Lafayette, California (unbuilt)
- Cameron Center Hotel, Palm Springs, California (unbuilt)
- De Anza Country Club clubhouse and residential master plan, Borrego Springs, California
- Desert Hills Hotel, Palm Springs, California
- Germains Liquor Store (for Sam Arner), Cathedral City, California
- John Gillin Residence, Thunderbird Country Club, Rancho Mirage, California
- Charles Hanson Residence, Tamarisk Country Club, Rancho Mirage, California
- Charles E. Jones Residence, Rancho Mirage, California
- George Kuhrts Residences #1 and 2 (for DiGiorgio Corp.), Borrego Springs, California
- Edwin Landsfield Residence, Deepwell Estates, Palm Springs, California
- La Quinta Desert Manor, La Quinta, California
- The Little Theatre, Rancho Mirage, California
- Marin Golf and Country Club and cottages (for Paul Trousdale and Associates), Novato, California (unbuilt)
- Marin Hotel and Sports Club (for Paul Trousdale and Associates), San Rafael, California (unbuilt)
- Rapid City Country Club Development Assoc. clubhouse, Rapid City, South Dakota
- Sigma Phi Epsilon fraternity house, University of Southern California, Los Angeles, California

Duane Wheeler Residence motor court, 1959, Indian Wells.

Jack and Joan Warde Residence, 1960, Indian Wells.

- The Springs Restaurant (remodel), Cameron Center, Palm Springs, California (no longer extant)
- Earle Strebe Residence (alteration), Palm Springs, California

**1958**
- Clarence and Marian Brown Residence, Eldorado Country Club Estates Cottages East #11-B (alteration), Indian Wells, California
- Cameron Center Mayfair Market and shops (for George Cameron, Jr.), Palm Springs, California
- Sidney Charney Residence, Tamarisk Country Club, Rancho Mirage, California (unbuilt)
- Residential plans for Tamarisk Country Club (for Art Coffey and George Ripley), Rancho Mirage, California
- Eldorado Country Club Master Plan, Estates and Cottages East, and temporary clubhouse (for Robert P. McCulloch), Indian Wells, California
- John Essig Residence, Cobb View Heights, California
- Lloyd R. French, Jr. Residence, Odessa, Texas
- Hotel and Restaurant (for William Gillander), Yucca Valley, California
- Charles Hansen Residence, Rancho Mirage, California
- Hi-Fidelity Unlimited retail complex, Menlo Park, California
- James J. Hines project, Pauma Valley, California
- Inglewood Country Club, Inglewood, California
- Lemurian Fellowship (remodel), Ramona, California
- Allen Lucas Residence, Woodside, California
- Northern Air Lodge and Country Club development, Scottsdale, Arizona
- Dr. Hampton Robinson's Medical Office Building, Houston, Texas
- St. Louis Catholic Church (alteration), Cathedral City, California
- Ronald Williams Residence #1 and 2, Eldorado Country Club Estates, Indian Wells, California

**1959**
- Charles Clare Residence, Tamarisk Country Club, Rancho Mirage, California
- Coronado Country Club Cottages, El Paso, Texas
- Eldorado Country Club clubhouse (with Ernest J. Kump & Associates, for Robert P. McCulloch), Indian Wells, California
- Hidden Shopping Center, (for Karl Lans), Hidden Springs, California
- Herbert E. Linden Residence, Eldorado Country Club Estates, Indian Wells, California

- Jack Mann Residence, Eldorado Country Club Estates Cottages West #34 (alteration), Indian Wells, California
- Palm Springs Spa (with Donald Wexler, Richard Harrison, and Philip Koenig, for Samuel W. Banowit), Palm Springs, California (no longer extant)
- Racquet Club clubhouse (alteration), Palm Springs, California
- Nat S. and Marian Rogers Residence, Eldorado Country Club Estates, Indian Wells, California
- Sydney and Evelyn Schiff Residence (addition), Racquet Club, Palm Springs, California
- Randolph and Patricia Scott Residence, Eldorado Country Club Estates Cottages West #36 (alteration), Indian Wells, California
- Mitchell Shepherd Residence, Eldorado Country Club Estates Cottages West #B-2 (alteration), Indian Wells, California
- Holmes and Virginia Tuttle Residence, Eldorado Country Club Estates Cottages West #A-3 (alteration), Indian Wells, California
- Frank Urbanek Residence, Indian Wells Country Club, Indian Wells, California
- Duane Wheeler Residence, Eldorado Country Club Estates, Indian Wells, California

**1960**
- Alexander Construction Company, Palm Springs, California
- Cameron Center Woolworths, Palm Springs, California
- Russell E. Chace Residence, Eldorado Country Club Estates Cottages West #38 (alteration), Indian Wells, California
- Desert Sun Shopping Center, Palm Springs, California
- Flagstaff Old Town hotel and shopping center, Flagstaff, Arizona
- Dr. Hampton C. Robinson Residence, Houston, Texas
- Palm Springs Mirror and Glass Company, Palm Springs, California
- Racquet Club Cottages West (for Paul Trousdale and Associates), Palm Springs, California
- Raymond J. Roger alteration, Palm Springs, California
- John Mc P. Rutherford apartment units, Twenty-Nine Palms, California
- John Mc P. Rutherford Residence, Twenty-Nine Palms, California
- Jack and Joan Warde Residence, Eldorado Country Club Estates, Indian Wells, California
- Mrs. Howard Standish Watson Residence, Palm Desert, California

Presentation drawings of Aloha Joe's entrance and interior with standing L-R, Lew Levy and Bill Cody, 1960. Aloha Joe's was one of two restaurants, along with Jeffrey's Cafe, that resulted from the remodeling of The Springs in the Cameron Center.

Rendering for Eldorado Cove Cottages, 1961, Indian Wells.

Crank and Garland Residence #2, bought before completion by Jack and Paula Petrie, 1962, Indian Wells (draftsman unknown).

**1961**

- Aloha Joe's and Jeffrey's Cafe, Palm Springs, California
- Robert and Betty Cannon Residence, Eldorado Country Club Estates, Indian Wells, California
- William and Winifred Cody Residence (remodel), Avalon, Catalina Island, California
- Fillmore Crank and Beverly Garland Residence #1, Desert Bel Air Estates, Indian Wells, California
- Eldorado Country Club Estates Cottages West and recreation area (for Robert P. McCulloch), Indian Wells, California
- Eldorado Cove Cottages West #1–8 (for Eugine E. Mance), Indian Wells, California
- Owen and Darlene Goodman Apartment Units, Palm Springs, California
- Ed Janss Residence, Eldorado Country Club Estates, Indian Wells, California
- La Fontana Marina and Hotel, Marina del Rey, California (unbuilt)
- Raymond Mithun Residence, Eldorado Country Club Estates, Indian Wells, California
- Louise Durham Nicoletti Residence, Thunderbird Heights, Rancho Mirage, California
- Palo Alto Hills Golf and Country Club, Palo Alto, California
- Round Hill Country Club clubhouse and service buildings, Alamo, California (no longer extant)
- Shell service station, Sunrise Way, Palm Springs, California (unbuilt)
- W. & J. Sloane Company display residence, La Quinta, California
- White House of the West, Eldorado Country Club Estates Cottages West, Indian Wells, California (built, used for different program)

**1962**

- James and Helen Abernathy Residence, Palm Springs, California
- Fillmore Crank and Beverly Garland Residence #2 (purchased before completion by Jack and Paula Petrie), Desert Bel Air Estates, Indian Wells, California
- Douglas Driggs Residence, Paradise Hills, Arizona
- Walter Dunivant Residence (for Fillmore Crank), Desert Bel Air Estates Development, Indian Wells, California
- George Eccles Cottage (alteration), Eldorado Country Club Estates Cottages East #6, Indian Wells, California
- Garrett Residence (alteration), Eldorado Country Club Estates, Indian Wells, California
- Willard Keith Residence, Eldorado Country Club Estates, Indian Wells, California
- Maurice L. Melamed Residence, Wonder Palms Estates, Tamarisk Country Club, Rancho Mirage, California
- Sollenberger Residence, Phoenix, Arizona
- Southridge Inc. model home/Stanley Goldberg Residence, Palm Springs, California
- Western Savings and Loan Branch (with Dailey and Associates, for Douglas Driggs), Tempe, Arizona

**1963**

- Robert and Betty Cannon Residence, Eldorado Country Club Estates Cottages West #6 (alteration), Indian Wells, California
- Henry Chaddick Residence (addition), Palm Springs, California
- Keith and Linda Gaede Residence (alteration and addition), Eldorado Country Club Estates, Indian Wells, California

Round Hill Country Club, 1961, Alamo, California. The poolside sunshade structure is redolent of Cody's shade structures for Eldorado Country Club recreation area, and for the Palm Springs Spa bathhouse colonnade and pool side canopies (delineated by J.R. Hollingsworth).

Shell Service Station, 1964 , Palm Springs.

William Siemon Residence, view from entry courtyard through house, 1963, Palm Springs.

The covered walkway to the front doors of the Dr. Henry L. Jaffe and Diana Gaines Residence is illuminated at night with floor lights. The poolside patio is on the right and a detached guest house is on the left; 1963, Rancho Mirage.

Model of Maurice L. Melamed Residence, 1962, Rancho Mirage.

Rendering of the entrance to La Quinta Country Club Clubhouse, 1964, La Quinta (unbuilt).

- Philip Goldman Residence, Desert Bel Air Estates, Indian Wells, California
- Harold Hirsh Residence, Wonder Estates, Rancho Mirage, California
- Dr. Henry L. Jaffe and Diana Gaines Residence, Rancho Mirage, California
- Joseph and Nelda Linsk Residence (addition), Palm Springs, California
- McCulloch Properties Inc. Cottages, Lake Havasu City, Arizona
- Ralph Ogden Residence, Eldorado Country Club Estates, Indian Wells, California
- The Palm Springs Spa Hotel (with Philip Koenig, for Samuel W. Banowit), Palm Springs, California (no longer extant)
- Palm Springs Spa Hotel doctor's suite (alteration), Palm Springs, California
- Palm Springs Tennis Club Deluxe bungalows (for Harry Chaddick), Palm Springs, California
- St. Theresa Master Plan (convent, church, school, and rectory), Palm Springs, California
- Paul J. Schmitt Residence, Eldorado Country Club Estates, Indian Wells, California
- Jennings B. and Anna Shamel Residence, Eldorado Country Club Estates, Indian Wells, California
- William Siemon Residence, Palm Springs, California
- Sky Mountain development, Rancho Mirage, California

### 1964
- Araby Point Hotel, Palm Springs, California
- Arthur Bailey (McFie) Residence (alteration), Smoke Tree Ranch, Palm Springs, California
- Fillmore Crank Sr. Residence, Paradise Valley, Arizona
- Desert Bel Air Estates residential development (for Fillmore Crank), Indian Wells, California
- Eldorado Properties (alteration and addition), Indian Wells, California
- Foster Store Building, Palm Springs, California
- John Kell Houssels, Jr. Residence, Las Vegas, Nevada
- Indian Springs Development (with Alfred Beadle), Rancho Mirage, California
- Irvine Beach Pavilion, Orange County, California
- La Quinta Country Club clubhouse, La Quinta, California (unbuilt)
- Joseph and Nelda Linsk Residence #2 (addition), Palm Springs, California
- Litchfield Park Apartments, (with Dailey and Associates), Litchfield Park, Arizona
- Horace W. McCurdy Residence, Eldorado Country Club, Indian Wells, California

- Palm Springs Tennis Club additional deluxe bungalows (for Harry Chaddick), Palm Springs, California
- Seven Lakes Country Club clubhouse, Palm Springs, California
- Shell service station, North Palm Springs, California
- Valley Wide Shopping Center Phases I and II, Palm Desert, California (unbuilt)
- Western Savings and Loan home office (with Alfred N. Beadle, Dailey and Associates for Douglas Driggs), Phoenix, Arizona

### 1965
- Jacques Clerk Residence, Eldorado Country Club Estates, Indian Wells, California
- Weir McDonald Residence, Paradise Valley, Arizona
- Palm Springs Spa Hotel Gymnasium, Palm Springs, California
- St. Theresa Convent, Palm Springs, California
- Tennis Club Homes development (for Harry Chaddick), Palm Springs, California

### 1966
- Cannon, Ted Munday and Associates Residence, Eldorado Country Club Estates, Indian Wells, California
- James C. Gruener Residence (alteration), Borrego Springs, California
- McCulloch Properties Inc. Building, Indian Wells, California
- Donald T. and Ann Randall Residence, Eldorado Country Club Estates, Indian Wells, California
- Frank Rusalem Residence (alteration), Palm Springs, California
- Town and Country Shopping Center (for Robert Dwyer), Palm Desert, California

### 1967
- Thomas J. and Arline Bannon Residence, Eldorado Country Club Estates, Indian Wells, California
- Central Plaza and Office Complex (for McCulloch Properties Inc.), Maricopa County, Arizona
- Dale Clark Residence (alteration), Smoke Tree Ranch, Palm Springs, California
- Chet Dolley Residence, Palm Springs, California
- Eldorado Country Club clubhouse dining room and bar (extension), Indian Wells, California
- Dr. Branch and Carol Kerfoot Residence, Newport Beach, California
- McCulloch Corporation main plant facility (for Robert P. McCulloch), Lake Havasu, Arizona (unbuilt)
- Robert P. and Basie McCulloch Residence, Lake Havasu City, Arizona, (unbuilt)

Seven Lakes Country Club Clubhouse, 1964, Palm Springs (delineated by J.R. Hollingsworth).

St. Theresa convent was financed by the Bob Hope family, 1965, Palm Springs.

Donald T. and Ann Randall Residence, 1966, Eldorado Country Club Estates, Indian Wells (purchased by John King, 1969).

Town & Country Office Building and Stores, 1966, Palm Desert.

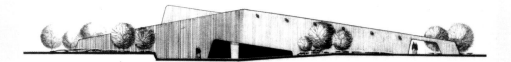

Central plaza and office complex includes a guest hotel & restaurant facility, 1967, Maricopa County, Arizona.

Palm Desert City Entrance Sign was built on land donated by Cody, part of his parcel for his new office at Valley Wide Center. The sign includes a Vietnam Memorial stone and three flagpoles flying the American flag, the California state flag, and the third reserved for the home flags of visiting foreign dignitaries.

McCulloch Corporation Main Plant Facility 1967, Lake Havasu, Arizona (unbuilt).

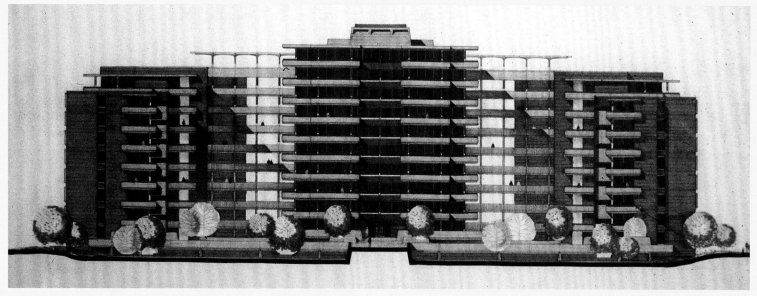

Eldorado West, a.k.a. Quivara front elevation of a multistory condominium and golf course development adjacent to the west side of Eldorado Country Club, 1969, Indian Wells (unbuilt).

- Robert P. and Basie McCulloch Residence (remodel and addition), Thunderbird Country Club, Rancho Mirage, California
- Comprehensive development plan for the Palm Springs Central Business District, by Palm Springs Planning Collaborative (Robson Chambers, John Porter Clark, William F. Cody, Albert Frey, Richard Harrison, Herman Ranes, E. Stewart Williams, H. Roger Williams), Palm Springs, California (unbuilt)
- Palm Springs sidewalk improvement, Palm Springs, California
- Albert Petrie Residence (alteration), Eldorado Country Club Estates, Indian Wells, California

**1968**
- City of Palm Desert Entrance Sign, Palm Desert, California
- City of Palm Springs Entrance Sign and Attraction Board, Palm Springs, California
- William and Barbara Foster Residence, Palm Springs, California
- Fountain Hills Page Ranch (for McCulloch Properties Inc.), Fountain Hills, Arizona
- Multiresidential project (for T. Hamilton), Lake Havasu City, Arizona
- James Killion Residence, Manitou Springs, Colorado
- Kohler Residence, Palm Springs, California
- Richard P. McCulloch Residence Playa del Rey, California
- Rhu House, Lemurian Fellowship, Ramona, California
- St. Theresa Catholic Church, Palm Springs, California
- Homer Scott Residence (alteration), Smoke Tree Ranch, Palm Springs, California
- Sherman's Delicatessen (former The Springs restaurant), Cameron Center (alteration and addition), Palm Springs, California (no longer extant)
- Starlite Development Inc. condominiums, Lake Havasu, Arizona
- Valley Wide Shopping Center apartment building, Palm Desert, California

**1969**
- Robert Brown Residence (formerly Shamel Residence, alteration), Eldorado Country Club Estates, Indian Wells, California
- Denver office tower (Cody-Martin Joint Venture), Denver, Colorado
- Desert Air Country Club clubhouse and condominiums (for Jimmy J. Hines), Rancho Mirage, California
- Eldorado West (Quivara) Golf Course and residential development (for General American Development Corp.), Indian Wells, California (unbuilt)
- 'The Fairway' Condominiums (for Morris Ebin), Tamarisk Country Club 10th Fairway, Rancho Mirage, California
- Robert Gibbs & Sons Realty Inc. Apartment Building, Lake Havasu City, Arizona
- Holmsted Apartments, Lake Havasu City, Arizona
- George Killion Residence, Eldorado Country Club Estates, Indian Wells, California
- John M. King Residence (formerly Donald and Ann Randall Residence, alteration and addition), Eldorado Country Club Estates, Indian Wells, California
- John M. King Residence (addition), Denver, Colorado
- Las Palmas Restaurant (for McCulloch Properties Inc.), Lake Havasu City, Arizona
- McCulloch Plaza (McCulloch Oil Corporation headquarters, \ computer center, and airport-marina industrial center at Los Angeles International Airport), Los Angeles, California (unbuilt)
- MGM Studios master plan (for Culver City Properties), Culver City, California, 1969
- Palm Springs Shopping Center Plaza North, Palm Springs, California
- Safari Golf Club clubhouse, Coachella Valley, California
- Silver Spur Golf Club and Housing, Palm Desert, California
- Max Stoffel Residence (remodel and addition), Southridge Estates, Palm Springs, California
- Stanley Weiner Residence, Tamarisk Country Club, Rancho Mirage, California
- T. Weiner Residence, Canyon Country Club, Palm Springs, California

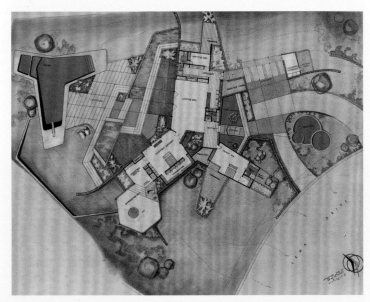

Floor Plan for Robert P. and Basie McCulloch's Hilltop Residence, 1967, Lake Havasu City, Arizona (unbuilt).

Desert Air Country Club Clubhouse, 1969, Rancho Mirage.

Silver Spur golf club and housing development, 1969, Palm Desert (delineated by Purciel).

Highland Park Community Activity Pavilion & Public Swim Complex, 1970, Palm Springs; a Palm Springs Architects' Collaborative project with William F. Cody in capacity as City Architect (delineated by Purciel).

Mexican elements are blended with modern design in the entry and foyer of the William and Barbara Foster Residence, 1968, Palm Springs. Courtesy of *Palm Springs Life*.

The Fairway condominiums on Tamarisk Country Club 10th fairway (renamed Cody Court), 1969, Rancho Mirage.

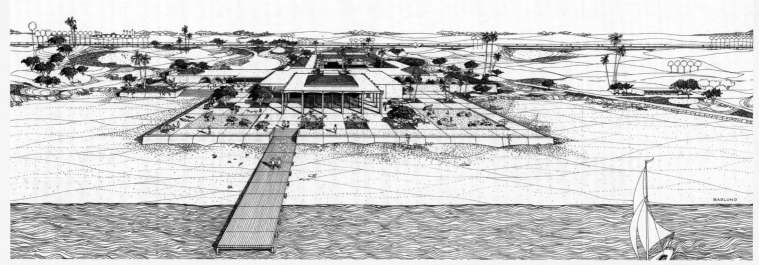

Clubhouse oceanfront approach for Puerto de Oro Country Club (Club de Oro) golf club, trailer park, beach facility, and pavilion building, 1971, Guadalajara, Mexico (rendering by Barlund).

## 1970

- Birmingham Civic Center (competition entry), Birmingham, Alabama, (unbuilt)
- Ely R. Callaway Jr. Residence, Eldorado Country Club Estates, Indian Wells, California
- Crane Residence, Eldorado Country Club Estates, Indian Wells, California
- James Killion Residence, Indian Wells Country Club, Indian Wells, California
- Palm Canyon Condominiums, Palm Springs, California
- Pavilion and public swimming pool complex (with Palm Springs Collaborative for Highlands Community Center), Palm Springs, California (unbuilt)

## 1971

- Arizona Snow Bowl Village lodge, spa club, tennis facilities, condominiums and entrance gates, (for Bruce Leadbetter & Warren Ridge) Flagstaff, Arizona
- Harry P. Barrand and Ann Kachlein Residence, Thunderbird Country Club, Rancho Mirage, California
- California State University San Bernardino Audio-Visual Library and classroom building (with Criley and McDowell), San Bernardino, California
- Deep Canyon Tennis Club, Palm Desert, California
- Indian Wells Racquet Club, Indian Wells, California
- Robert P. McCulloch Residence (alteration), Thunderbird Country Club, Rancho Mirage, California
- Ralph Ogden Residence Eldorado Country Club Estates (pool enclosure), Indian Wells, California
- Palm Canyon Village Multi-Residential Development, Palm Springs, California
- Palm Residence landscape plan, Rancho Mirage, California
- Puerto de Oro (Club de Oro) Country Club master plan (golf course, trailer park, beach facility, and pavilion), Guadalajara, Mexico
- Joseph L. Stone Residence (alteration), Tamarisk Country Club, Rancho Mirage, California
- Union Hills development (for George Killion), Phoenix, Arizona,

## 1972

- Andreas Hills Condominiums Phase II (a Tennis Club development for Harry Chaddick), Palm Springs, California
- Canyon Hotel (addition), Palm Springs, California
- Desert Hospital landscape design, Palm Springs, California
- Maui Continental Hotel and condominiums, Lahaina, Maui, Hawaii (unbuilt)
- Hotel at Los Angeles International Airport (for Robert P. McCulloch), Los Angeles, California (unbuilt)
- Samuel and Gladys Rubinstein Residence, Rancho Mirage, California
- Charles R. Warde Residence, Eldorado Country Club Estates, Indian Wells, California
- Whitewater Country Club clubhouse and condominiums (a Tennis Club development for Harry Chaddick), Palm Springs, California

## 1973

- Palm Springs Tennis Club Hotel (for Harry Chaddick), Palm Springs, California

## 1974

- Club de Golf Santa Anita Country Club (with Jaime Gomez, Vazquez Aldana Associates and Lawrence Hughes, course designer), Guadalajara, Mexico

## 1975

- Palm Springs Public Library (with Sheehy and John Cody), Palm Springs, California
- George and Kathy Pardee Residence (with Sheehy and John Cody), Eldorado Country Club Estates, Indian Wells, California
- Ed Riback Residence (with Sheehy and John Cody), Tamarisk Country Club, Rancho Mirage, California

Arizona Snow Bowl Village, 1971, Flagstaff, Arizona.

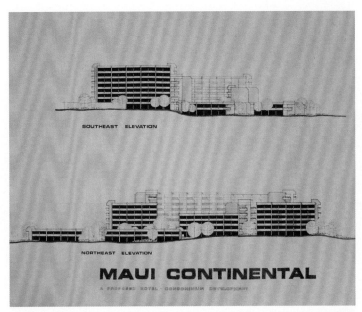

Maui Continental Hotel and Condominium Development, 1972, Lahaina, Maui, Hawaii (unbuilt, delineated by Purciel).

Club de Golf Santa Anita Country Club, included the master plan for a recreational and multiresidential development including a clubhouse; with associate architects Jaime Gomez, Vazquez Aldana & Associates, and golf course designer Lawrence Hughes, 1974, Guadalajara, Mexico.

Ed Riback Residence front elevation, Cody/Sheehy/Cody Architects, 1975, Rancho Mirage.

# *My Father, William F. Cody*

Catherine Cody

My dad's close friend and colleague, A. Quincy Jones, once remarked, "Bill Cody was a spirited, generous man as well as innovative in his architecture. All of this certainly comes through in the character of his work." This sentiment is shared by many who knew him. These qualities, as well as his jolly personality accompanied by a constant belly laugh, is how I remember him. If you couldn't find him, you could hear him! His optimism and sense of humor were a joy to know. I don't remember what he looked like without a smile. His friend John Vogley remembered, "Ahead of seeing him, you knew he was there. Bill's exuberant laughter was infectious. He lived his life fully, Bill Cody's way." Along with his incorrigible positive attitude, dad saw the beauty in life around him, in people and in creating architecture.

My dad's work was rooted in his closeness to family. He continued the mentorship that began with his mother Anna, and in turn mentored his brother Jay to become an architect. When Jay recovered from tuberculosis in 1954, dad invited him to move to Palm Springs and work in his office while he guided him to develop his career.

He was curious and open; interested in reading about history and the natural world, as well as advancements in science and medicine, and sharing ideas with innovative thinkers. The way that my parents raised me and my two sisters reflected their passions: creative work, friendships, entertaining, and travel—and he combined these whenever he could. Not counting the professional and family trips that were so important to him, all of the things he loved about life came together in the house that he built for his family, completed a few years ahead of when I was born. Our home also served as a showcase for clients and

friends; it had to be perfect and was built without compromising my father's high standards.

Our house was completed the same year as the L'Horizon bungalow hotel, which dad designed for Jack Wrather and Bonita Granville, producers of the legendary television series *Lassie* and *The Lone Ranger*. For a housewarming gift, the Wrathers gave our family a collie puppy who came from the same breeder as the dogs who played Lassie. My parents named him Beau.

Growing up, much of the social and business scene of Palm Springs evolved around golf, tennis, and cocktail parties. Dad didn't have time to play golf or tennis, although he was a lifetime member of the clubs he designed. Our family enjoyed the clubs' amenities; often while my mom played golf, my dad attended business luncheons, and together they enjoyed the evening cocktail parties.

My parents liked entertaining and we often hosted barbecues at our home. The configuration of the house lent itself to large gatherings, with the sliding glass doors fully open to merge the living room with the patio. The house's interior illumination was complemented from the lawn area by tiki torches and garden lights that created dramatic silhouettes. When a guest would play our piano, my mom, who had sung professionally before she married my dad, would captivatingly sing along.

Party menus didn't vary much from the thick steaks marinated in garlic salt, rosemary, and soy sauce, served with sautéed mushrooms and onions, a baked potato topped with butter, sour cream, and chives, a

Bill and Jay Cody at Lake Tahoe, c. 1936.

Bill and Wini (top row, second from right and far right); Bill drew his mustache on the print, c. 1940.

Bill and Wini surveying the property for our Palm Springs house, c. 1946.

Model of the Cody Residence, c. 1946–48.

Bill with Diane (l), and Lynne (r) at our house's construction site, c. 1950.

Bill with Diane (l) on her 7th birthday and Lynne (r) outside the bungalow on East Tahquitz Way, Palm Springs, c. 1951.

Bill (holding Lynne), Diane, and Wini in Phoenix, c. 1951.

Our collie Beau outside the living room and our parents' bedroom, 1953.

Bill with client in Monterrey, Mexico, c. 1956.

salad, and toasted garlic bread. Herb Albert and the Tijuana Brass, Ella Fitzgerald, Nat King Cole and other jazz musicians, as well as bossa nova and mariachi music, played on the turntable. The voices and laughter would crescendo over the music. These were truly memorable events!

We also had large annual holiday office parties. Dad brought people together from all walks of life; his staff, friends, clients, and anyone he met during the year that made a difference in his life; people who otherwise may not have crossed paths. Dad was generous and he always tried to let people know he appreciated them. Our housekeeper Lucinda came not to help but enjoy the party with her husband, Lacy. The common thread was being a friend to Bill, and it was his way to thank everyone for the year. As a youngster, I couldn't see through crowd, but I could follow his laughter and easily found him. His larger-than-life and gregarious personality was welcoming to everyone.

Dad's passion for his work was strong and he loved his family. Ideally, he would have liked us all to be with him at the office. When not in school, it was the most fun place to be. At lunch, we went next door to Mayfair market (in the Cameron Center that he had designed), for snack foods: Euphrates sesame crackers, Muenster cheese, salami rounds, Dijon mustard, Lay's Barbecue potato chips, Boston peanuts, Abba-Zaba candy bars, and varieties of Wrigley chewing gum with Fanta and Squirt sodas to wash it down. We would sit at a corner of his desk while we consumed our bounty.

There were other ways that we got caught up in his work, even as children. He didn't think twice about taking me to planning commission meetings. I remember going to a meeting at City Hall, where all of the allotted chairs around the conference table were assigned. My dad borrowed a chair from the hall and set it next to him for me. City officials came in wearing their business attire with attaché cases. Not complying with such standard conventions, dad, was in a sports shirt and, like me, wearing Go Ahead flip-flops. We looked like we'd just come off the beach. Dad wasn't self-conscious about any of it.

My father loved to travel and family trips were opportunities for us to learn about the world and architecture. Two cross-country road trips included visits to his mother's sisters, Philomena and Edith, in Philadelphia, once in August 1952 with my sisters, and again in June 1965 on our way to attend Dad's induction into the AIA College of Fellows. Both trips included stopping to visit national monuments and historic landmarks along the way.

My parents also traveled on their own to Europe, but it was a major family trip when I was 15 that really opened my eyes. Diane and Lynne started separately on a student tour to the Scandinavian countries, while my parents, myself, and a family friend flew to London. Dad bought a blue Volkswagen Squareback and we toured England, then ferried over to Calais and drove on to Paris, then through the Alps to Milan, Venice, Florence, and Rome (where we saw *Aida* performed in the Baths of Caracalla); on to the former Yugoslavia, down the Dalmatian Coast, to Diocletian's Palace in Split and the walled city of Dubrovnik in Croatia, and then to Greece. In Athens we saw the ruins of the Parthenon, agoras, and theaters. We took a five-day cruise of the Greek islands including Mykonos, the ruins of Mycenae on Crete, and then when we returned

Cathy at the beach, Avalon, Catalina Island, 1956.

Bill in Seville, Spain, 1960.

(l-r) Bill with Jay Cody and Per Toft, c. 1961.

Cody Residence, view from dining table toward primary bedroom through the living room, c. 1961.

Cody Residence, view from dining area toward living room, conversation pit, and atrium with the center-pivot door to the children's bedroom (later, the library) on the right, c. 1961.

Bill and Wini in the atrium in front of mosaic wall, c. 1962.

to Athens we drove to Istanbul where we visited the Hagia Sophia and Topkapı Palace. From Istanbul, dad shipped the car home and we flew to our last stop, Amsterdam, before flying home. Traveling with dad was an amazing adventure. As always, he was endlessly enthusiastic and optimistic, easily making friends along the way. He knew the history of our destinations, especially the architecture, making our touring all the more interesting. We often didn't have hotel reservations and meandered until late in the days to see as much as we could along the way. He wanted to show us the best trip that he could, and he did! Incidentally, when the Volkswagen arrived home, dad gifted it to an employee from the Philippines who, along with his family, he had sponsored to live and work in the US.

But it was travel closer to home that became another important center for our family. In 1956, my parents began taking us for summers to Avalon on Santa Catalina Island, which was closer than their other destination of choice, Lake Tahoe. Dad would work during the week and join us on weekends. After renting houses for a few years, in 1959 my father's office manager Richard Wilson found a rare opportunity for my parents to purchase a two-story house with a large garden, which became our vacation home. Dad remodeled it and divided it into two apartments; the upstairs was for our family and he leased out the bottom unit. Beginning in 1968 until my dad's stroke, my parents hosted

an annual meeting of the California Council Women's Architecture League and California Council of the American Institute of Architects in Avalon. These September events coincided with the Catalina Arts Festival, when the main pedestrian promenade was lined with artwork. On Friday night after checking in their hotel, guests would come up to the house for an evening cocktail party lit by tiki torches in the garden, and again on Saturdays for a barbecue dinner.

I never knew my dad to fear anything except doctor appointments with his cardiologist, Dr. George Kaplan, whom dad respected but was inured to repeated reprimands to change his lifestyle habits. However, my dad's driven and irrepressible personality caught up with him in early spring of 1973, with a devastating stroke that broke his invincible spirit along with his body. The left side of his body was left paralyzed and he was constrained to a wheelchair until he passed away five-and-a-half years later.

Because of his illness he was no longer able to draw, which devastated him. Our family, devoted friends, and dad's colleagues, including Bob Stevens in Fresno and George Hasslein in San Luis Obispo, encouraged and engaged with dad as much as possible to try to lift his spirits. A. Quincy and Elaine Jones sent my father get well cards every day during his recovery in the hospital and after he got home. His office's projects

Wini and Bill at Eldorado Country Club, 1962.

Bill and Wini dancing at Eldorado Country Club, 1964.

Bill in his Palm Springs office, 1965.

Cody family portrait: (back row, l-r) Bill, Diane, and Lynne; (front row) Wini and Cathy, 1966.

Bill in Lindos, Rhodes, Greece, 1969.

Bill in Amsterdam, 1969.

continued to receive recognition and awards. He was emotional with gratitude, but sad that he couldn't produce more architecture.

After my dad died, we knew that we would have to preserve his important architectural legacy, and this book is a culmination of that very long effort. But all of his exceptional work cannot encompass the wonderful, gifted person he was—my father and friend to so many, William F. Cody.

Bill with (l-r) Wini, Lynne, Diane, and Cathy in front of St. Theresa Church, Jim and Pam Riley wedding, June 21, 1975.

Bill with the model of the Robert P. and Basie McCulloch Residence.

Bill with the McCulloch Residence model.

Bill on the deck of summer home on Catalina Island, 1972.

# Biographical Timeline

**July 15, 1915**
Anna Elizabeth Shadle (1887–1977), an interior decorator and artist, marries William F. Cody (Sr.) (1873–1944), owner of a chain of nine haberdashery stores in Illinois and Ohio.

**June 19, 1916**
William (Bill) Francis Cody, Jr. is born in Dayton, Ohio.

**April 16, 1919**
Anna Elizabeth Jr., born and dies five hours later. This loss, and Bill's early onset of asthma, prompts William Cody, Sr. to sell his business and move the family to Los Angeles, California.

**1920–1924**
The Cody family rents a bungalow in the Jefferson Park neighborhood. Anna designs a development of bungalows, demonstrating her drafting abilities to her young son, and the family moves into one of them at 3745 W. 27th Street.

**1925**
John James Monroe (Jay) is born May 14, 1925. Shortly after Jay's birth, the Cody family moves to Beverly Hills.

While living in Beverly Hills, Anna designs a two-story Spanish style home for the family on Midvale Avenue in Westwood Hills. Anna teaches Bill about the design and drafting of plans for the new residence. Anna designs and Bill assists with carving and painting the overdoor panels.

**1927**
Bill, eleven years old, collaborates on the design of the next family home with Anna on Kearsarge Street, Brentwood Heights.

**1928–1930**
Bill meets his future wife, Winifred (Wini) Allyne Smith, in 8th grade at Hawthorne School.

**1931**

January 31, 1931

As part of the winter class of 1930, Bill and Wini graduate from the Hawthorne School at the Beverly Vista school auditorium; Bill is on the left end, Wini is fifth from right.

**1931–1934**

Bill and Wini attend Beverly Hills High School. Bill designs stage sets and delineates his designs for the Drama Department's performances, and is illustrator for the school newspaper.

Bill's stage design for Beverly Hills High School 1934 senior class production of *A Merry, Mad, Modern Comedy*. Wini Smith was also in the cast.

Built set for *A Merry, Mad, Modern Comedy*, photograph by Don Milton, Beverly Hills.

**January 31, 1934**

Bill and Wini graduate in the Twelfth Commencement of Beverly Hills High School.

Bill's high school graduation portrait, 1934.

**1935**

Bill apprentices for the architectural firm of Heth Wharton and for architect William Asa Hudson.

Bill with William F. Cody, Sr.

**1936**

Bill continues working for Hudson until college while developing his own career as an independent designer and draftsman working from his family home in Brentwood Heights.

Two of Bill's important clients with whom he works with during this period include developer L.H. Pickens Co. and the Keith Apartment and Hotel Company.

Bill begins what is to become a long association as a designer and draftsperson for visionary developer Cliff May, whose Sunset Boulevard office was very near Cody's home studio in Brentwood. Recognizing Cody's talent as an artist and designer, May hires Cody to develop residential designs including ranch houses, forming a significant working alliance that continues beyond Cody's college career.

**1938–1940**

Bill attends Santa Monica Junior College (now Santa Monica College).

In the summer of 1939, Bill journeys to Guatemala, El Salvador, and Honduras. In Honduras, he meets Dr. Hector Valenzuela, who will become a major client two years later.

**1940**

Portrait of Bill taken at his mother's parents' studio in York, Pennsylvania, c. 1940.

With a junior college degree in hand, Bill enters the School of Architecture and Fine Arts at the University of Southern California as a sophomore at the beginning of the winter semester.

Bill joins several associated fraternities at USC: Upsilon fraternity; Tau Sigma Delta fraternity; Scarab fraternity; and Alpha Rho Chi fraternity. He meets John Hollingsworth, a sophomore, and Edward Killingsworth, a senior, both of whom would become lifelong friends. In the ensuing years, Hollingsworth becomes a technical illustrator and renders several presentation drawings for Bill's projects, and Killingsworth becomes a noted California modernist architect.

**1941**

Bill is selected by Delta Phi Delta, an honorary fine arts fraternity, where he serves as president during his senior year. He meets George Hasslein, who would become a close friend and would go on to be the founding dean of the College of Architecture & Environmental Design at California Polytechnic State University, San Luis Obispo, California.

June 5: Professor of Architecture V.L. Annis writes a letter to the Armed Forces requesting Bill's deferment of enlisting until after he graduates the following year. In support of Bill's deferment, Professor Annis states: "Mr. Cody is one of a very small group of unquestioned leaders, and pace-setters, in the next year's graduating class. Mr. Cody is one of the most promising men in his professional qualifications that we have had in several years."

Hired by W.A. Bechtel Co. Engineers and Contractors as designer and head draftsman for dormitories and school buildings in Morenci, Arizona, Bill induces USC classmates Howard Morgridge (left) and Bob Stevens (middle) to accompany him on the job. Summer 1941, Morenci, Arizona.

August 29: Bill travels to Tegucigalpa, Honduras to design a large Residence for Dr. Hector Valenzuela.

**1942**

June 6: Bill receives his Bachelor of Architecture from USC College of Architecture and Fine Arts. Among graduates are Cody's lifelong friends Eldon Davis, Howard Morgridge, and Bob Stevens.

In October, Bill, George Hasslein, and fourteen USC students from Professor Whitney Smith's class work on the Master Plan design for the City of Victorville, including Victor Union High School, parks, housing and highways.

On November 11, Bill enlists in the U.S. Navy Reserves as Apprentice Seaman; class V-II, for four years. The following month, Bill is given a Special Discharge from the U.S. Navy Reserves on the basis that he did not meet "approved standards for appointment" because of physical conditions and asthma.

**1943**

Bill's begins to design projects in the San Francisco Bay area. He moves to Oakland at the beginning of the year to work for Donald R. Warren Co. on the Fontana Steel Plant and other projects.

Later in the year he designs and drafts plans for Navy installations for Treasure Island and outlying bases for Blanchard Maher, and Ward Architects, San Francisco, as well as working on projects in the Los Angeles area for Cliff May and begins an alliance with Marsh, Smith and Powell, Architects.

Bill and Wini marry in Oakland on July 31.

Bill and Wini's wedding, July 31, 1943.

Bill and Wini's wedding party. Top row (l-r): Wini's father, Fred Smith; unknown; Bill's mother, Anna Cody; Wini's mother, Mildred Bartley. Bottom row (l-r): Bill's father, William Cody, Sr.; unknown; Bill; Wini; Bill's brother, Jay Cody (Bill's best man).

## 1944

Bill opens an office at 11975 Santa Monica Boulevard in West Los Angeles and works as head designer for Marsh, Smith and Powell, Architects. He executes the design and site plans for elementary schools, high schools, music buildings, UCLA administration and maintenance buildings, the University of Redlands Life Science Building, and numerous commercial projects.

Before Bill and Wini fully move to their apartment in Santa Monica, Diane Louise Cody is born in San Francisco on March 14, 1944.

Wini with Diane Cody, 1944.

## 1945

Bill is awarded the design for the Flagstaff High School and Gymnasium by the Flagstaff (Arizona) School District. He partners with Phoenix firm Gilmore & Varney.

## 1946

Bill becomes a fully licensed architect in California, May 10.

July: Bill opens an office at 401 W. Adams Street in Phoenix for his Arizona projects.

Bill in front of his West Los Angeles office, c. 1946.

Bill in his office, with a drawing of the Aherne/Fontaine residence (1943) for Cliff May on the wall in the background.

Bill designs the Flagstaff Elementary and Dunbar Elementary Schools in Flagstaff, Arizona, partnering with Gilmore & Varney.

The Codys move to Palm Springs as their permanent residence, renting a bungalow at 140 E. Tahquitz Canyon Way.

Bill is hired as staff architect for the Desert Inn Hotel by Nellie N. Coffman.

Bill and Wini purchase the lots to build their home from developer Paul Belding and Bill begins to design their house.

December 31, Bill acquires Arizona architecture license.

**1947**

Bill begins to receive increasingly high-profile commissions: the Del Marcos Apartment Hotel and Dorothy Levin residence in Palm Springs and the Haines Interior Studio and Offices, Beverly Hills.

Completion of Del Marcos Apartment Hotel, Palm Springs.

Completion of Dorothy Levin Residence, Palm Springs.

**1948**

April 29: Bill and Wini complete the purchase of their Desert Palms Estates' lots and begin the long process of building their home.

Bill opens what would become his main office in the building of realtor Russell Wade at 850 S. Palm Canyon Drive, Palm Springs.

June 17: The Codys' second daughter, Winifred Lynne (Lynne), is born in Santa Monica.

Bill with daughters Diane and Lynne at the Tahquitz Canyon Way bungalow home in Palm Springs, 1948.

August 14: Bill becomes a member of the American Institute of Architects (AIA).

**1949**

Bill is commissioned to design a golf club and residential development master plan at Thunderbird Ranch for developer John Dawson. Collaborating with golf course architect Lawrence Hughes, their design creates the first fairway-facing residential golf club development.

Completion of Haines Studio and Offices in Beverly Hills.

Completion of Spec Houses 1 and 2 for Fidler-Zagon Investment Corporation, Desert Palms Estates, Palm Springs.

Completion of the Dr. Robert A. Franklyn Residence, Los Angeles.

Completion of Our Lady of Malibu Catholic Church, Malibu.

**1950**

Bill's design of the Del Marcos Hotel included in the 1950 Britannica Yearbook.

Cody's design for the Dorothy Levin residence is included at an exhibition at Scripps College, Claremont, California: "Sixteen Southern California Architects Exhibit Contemporary Trends in a Group Showing at Scripps College."

**1951**

Five projects designed by Bill are included in *A Guide to Contemporary Architecture in Southern California,* with photographs by Julius Shulman and designed by Alvin Lustig: Our Lady of Malibu Church, Fidler-Zagon Investment Corp house, Dorothy Levin residence, Del Marcos Apartment Hotel, and the McFie residence.

Completion of Residential Master Plan & Thunderbird Country Club Clubhouse, Rancho Mirage.

Completion of Walt and Lily Disney Residence, Smoke Tree Ranch, Palm Springs.

**1952**

Bill designs the Mission Valley Country Club, a middle-income private golf club in San Diego for the Thunderbird Country Club team of John Dawson and Larry Hughes.

Completion of William and Winifred Cody Residence, Palm Springs.

Completion of L'Horizon Hotel, Palm Springs.

Completion of William Perlberg and Bobbe Brox Residence, Palm Springs.

Completion of Tamarisk Country Club Clubhouse.

**1953**

Selected projects of Bill are featured in Japan's World's Contemporary Architecture (vols. 2 and 4), Shokokusha Publishing Company.

William F. Cody business card, c. 1953.

March: The Cody family are fully moved into their new completed home on Desert Palms Drive, Palm Springs.

Bill opens an office at 1265 Rosecrans Avenue, San Diego, which he maintains until 1957.

Completion of La Jollan Hotel.

**1954**
After a long recovery from pulmonary tuberculosis, Bill's younger brother Jay moves to Palm Springs to apprentice with Bill. Their mother Anna also moves to Palm Springs.

June 20, the Cody's third daughter, Catherine (Cathy) Louise, is born in Santa Monica. The family spends the summer in La Jolla and commutes between his San Diego and Palm Springs offices.

Bill with daughters Lynne (left) and Cathy (right) at home in Palm Springs, 1955.

Bill travels to Havana multiple times to work on the Villa Real Country Club and Hotel, and the Edificio Mateal apartment and office building for Mexican developers María Teresa and Álvaro Gonzáles Gordon. Plans are executed for both Havana commissions but the projects were never built.

Completion of Mission Valley Country Club, San Diego, California.

Bill meets architect Henry H. Hester in San Diego after the completion of Mission Valley Country Club and Hester assists with managing the Villa Real Golf Hotel, supervising residential projects for Bill in San Diego.

**1955**
Bill continues to travel to Havana to work with the Mexican developers, the Gordons, on their projects. Plans are executed for both Havana commissions but were never built.

Bill and Wini in Las Vegas en route to Havana, 1955.

Completion of Earle and Marion Jorgensen Residence, Rancho Mirage.

Completion of Thunderbird Country Club Cottages, Rancho Mirage.

**1956**
Completion of Cameron Center Springs Restaurant, Palm Springs.

**1957**
Bill closes his San Diego office and opens an office on Pier 7 at the Embarcadero, San Francisco for a large low-income housing project in Contra Costa County. Architect Henry Hester moves with his wife to the Bay Area to partner with Bill on the project. Torrential rains flood several of the project sites and the development falls through. Hester moves back to San Diego and Bill keeps the San Francisco office open while securing other Bay Area projects.

Landscape architect John N. Vogley, a recent college graduate, arrives at the San Francisco office inquiring about renting space. Bill recognizes John's talent and invites him to stay. Bill assigns John to his first large landscape job: the Eldorado Country Club. Vogley will go on to work with Bill on numerous future projects.

**1958**

Bill designs two of his largest desert projects—the Eldorado Country Club Clubhouse and the Palm Springs Spa Bathhouse—simultaneously.

Completion 1958–59 of Eldorado Country Club Master Plan; Cottages East Estates and Clubhouse, Indian Wells.

**1959**
Completion of Palm Springs Spa Bathhouse.

**1960**

Introduction and publicity pages from Bill's 1960 projects portfolio.

From May 1960 through April 1965, Bill is a member of the Palm Springs Planning Commission, lending his expertise and voice to the development of important city zoning and ordinance regulations. He assists in developing a unique method of determining a building's height requirement in relationship to preserving its surrounding open space.

Bill meets visionary architects Buckminster Fuller and Paolo Soleri when they commune as guest lecturers at Cal Poly San Luis Obispo. Bill admires their different styles of ingenuity and creative thinking regarding housing development and environmental efficiency. In the ensuing years, Bill meets with Fuller in Southern California, and with Soleri at Arcosanti in Arizona.

Completion of Racquet Club Cottages West, Palm Springs.

Completion of Jack and Joan Warde Residence, Indian Wells.

Greek shipping magnate Aristotle Onassis engages Bill to discuss a joint venture with Prince Rainier of Monaco for the expansion of the existing Royal Golf Club, new country club, and a casino in southern France. Bill and Wini plan their first trip to Europe to meet with Prince Rainier. Landscape architect John Vogley is designated to attend the meeting, where he will travel with his wife Wynne.

From October 19 to December 7, the entourage travels throughout Europe, visiting London, Dublin, Paris, Amsterdam, Berlin, Frankfurt, Munich, Salzburg, Vienna, Geneva, Milan, Venice, Rome, Monte Carlo, Barcelona, Madrid, Seville, and Granada and seeing many of the most important examples of architecture in each.

Wini and Bill in Rome, 1960.

On November 22, Bill and John meet Prince Rainier's representative, and together they visit the Royal Golf Club. Bill and John discuss their expansion and landscaping ideas of the club, but the project dissolves when Onassis and Rainier part ways.

**1961**
Completion of Cameron Shopping Center, Palm Springs.

Bill opens an annex office on the north side of the newly completed Woolworths building in the Cameron Center, adjacent to his main office in Palm Springs.

Bill reviewing plans at his main office c. 1961 with Per Toft (with pipe) and Del Fiock, a custom hardware fabricator (behind Bill's right shoulder).

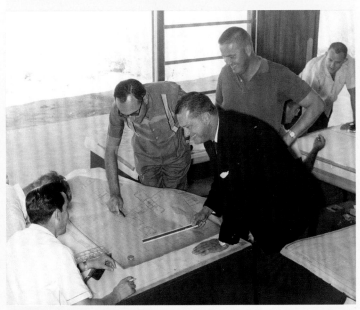

Bill reviewing plans at his annex office, with Jay Cody and associate Ira Johnson behind him, c. 1961. At Bill's suggestion, Jay moves to Los Angeles to gain experience working for other architects. Jay works in the office of Bill's friend William Pereira in Newport Beach. He also studies structural engineering with William Porush, a structural engineer employed by the Cody office.

Completion of Palo Alto Hills Golf and Country Club; residence for Robert and Betty Cannon and Eldorado Cottages West Estates, Indian Wells; residence for Louise Durham Nicoletti, Rancho Mirage; and show house for W. & J. Sloane Company, La Quinta.

### 1962
In April Bill and Wini visit Greenland, Denmark, Germany, Belgium, France, Italy, and England, coinciding with the USC alumni tour.

Jay Cody returns to Palm Springs to work in the primary office.

Completion of model residence for Southridge Inc. (Stanley Goldberg Residence), Palm Springs.

Completion of James and Helen Abernathy Residence, Palm Springs.

Completion of Douglas Driggs Residence, Paradise Hills, Arizona.

Completion of Western Savings & Loan, Tempe, Arizona.

### 1963
Completion of Palm Springs Spa Hotel.

Completion of Jennings B. and Anna Shamel Residence, Indian Wells.

Completion of Dr. Henry L. Jaffe and Diana Gaines Residence, Rancho Mirage.

Model of the proposed Palm Springs Central Business District.

April: Bill initiates and serves as chairman (until 1968) of the Palm Springs Planning Collaborative, including architects Robson Chambers, John Porter Clark, Albert Frey, Richard A. Harrison, H. Roger Williams, and Stewart Williams and city planner Herman Ranes. The purpose of the organization is to revitalize the central business district. To this end, Bill assists in formulating the zoning ordinances that help characterize the redevelopment plans of the city.

Completion of Western Savings & Loan Main Branch, Phoenix, Arizona.

Completion 1961–64 of the Desert Bel Air Estates Residential Development, Indian Wells.

### 1965
June 18: Bill is inducted into the College of Fellows of the American Institute of Architects at the Sheraton Park Hotel in Washington for his notable contribution to the advancement of the profession of architecture by his achievement in design. Bill's work is judged to have by its distinction, individuality and mastery of the art of design. Among the 15 photographs of examples of his work submitted for review were Eldorado Country Club, Palm Springs Spa Hotel and Bath House, and his own residence.

Completion of Weir McDonald Residence, Paradise Valley, Arizona.

### 1966
January: the Inland California Chapter of the AIA is granted to include Riverside and San Bernardino Counties, and Pomona Valley. Bill joins as a corporate member of the chapter, and is elected chapter vice president.

Jay receives his California architecture license in 1966 and Bill makes him an associate. Later, Jay becomes a partner in the practice.

Completion 1963–66 of Palm Springs Tennis Club Projects: Bungalows phases 1 and 2, Tennis Club Homes, Palm Springs.

**1967**

Bill is elected president of the Inland Chapter of the AIA.

While president of the Inland Chapter of the AIA, Bill forms the California Council Women's Architectural League (CCWAL). Wini Cody serves as the first president. W.A.L. members organize fund raising events and architectural tours to raise money for continued education.

Completion of Branch and Carol Kerfoot Residence, Newport Beach.

**1968**
January 20: The Inland Chapter of the AIA recognizes Bill with "appreciation for service" for his tenure as the 1967 Chapter President.

October 8: While Wini serves as president, the California Council Women's Architectural League meets in San Francisco.

December 8: The AIA's and Women's Architectural League (W.A.L.) host a home tour of four residences in Palm Springs, two of which are Cody projects: the Linsk residence alterations and the Goldberg residence.

Completion of St. Theresa Catholic Church, Palm Springs.

Completion of Rhu House, Lemurian Fellowship, Ramona, California.

**1969**
The Palm Springs Cody office maintains a staff varying from twelve to thirty technical employees consistent with production requirements, asserting itself as "the largest practice in the Coachella Valley area."

Bill teaching an architecture design studio class at Cal Poly San Luis Obispo, where for years he was an invited lecturer for the architecture department, c. 1969.

Bill plans an office at Lake Havasu City, Arizona, while working on projects for Robert McCulloch and others in the new developing community.

Bill becomes a member of the Architectural Guild for the Advancement of the University of Southern California School of Architecture.

**1970**
Cody office principals comprise Bill, Jay Cody, Laszlo Sandor, and Pat Sheehy.

Bill is elected the City Architect for the Palm Springs Collaborative, Inc. Members also include Jay Cody, Patrick Sheehy, Donald Wexler, Richard Harrison, Michael Black, David Hamilton, Wendell Veith, and Hugh M. Kaptur. The collaborative develops proposals for projects for Highland Park. Planned community recreational buildings were designed but only Bill's design for the Palm Springs Main Library was built.

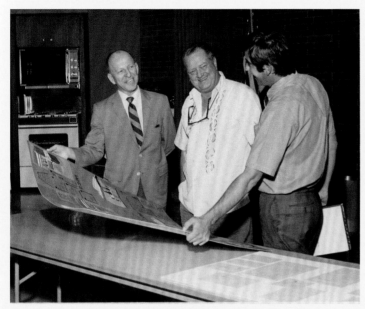

Bill (center) reviewing a design with junior partner Patrick Sheehy (right) and unidentified man, c. 1970.

August: Bill and Wini, along with their close friends, architect A. Quincy Jones and his wife Elaine, travel to Macau for an AIA convention and continue to Japan to visit Tokyo, they attend the Expo '70 in Suita, visit Osaka, and make a last stop in Thailand.

AIA group photo arriving in Macau, with Bill waving a hat and Wini in the center back with dark glasses and a printed blouse; 1970.

**1971**
Bill is invited to sit on the jury for the Pasadena AIA Chapter Honors Award Program.

Completion of California State University San Bernardino Audio-Visual Library and classroom building San Bernardino, California.

**1972**
Completion of Samuel and Gladys Rubinstein residence, Rancho Mirage, and Andreas Hills Condominium Development and Whitewater Country Club, Palm Springs.

**1973**
Cody office principals: Bill, Jay Cody, and Pat Sheehy.

In the spring of 1973, Bill suffers a debilitating stroke, leaving him wheelchair-bound and without the use of his hands to draw.

From one of the encouraging cards that Bill receives is a Christmas greeting from Dean George Hasslein of the College of Architecture and Environmental Design, Cal Poly San Luis Obispo, and his wife Jeanne.

April 16–20, 1979: An exhibition of the work of William F. Cody is held at the Architecture Gallery, Cal Poly San Luis Obispo, curated and designed by seniors Doug Fisher and Philip Dagort. Wini and daughters attend the exhibition.

Students in an elementary class at St. Theresa school sent handmade "get well" cards to Bill while he was in the hospital. This is the front and back of one of the children's cards.

**1974**
Completion of Club de Golf Santa Anita Country Club, Guadalajara, Mexico.

**1975**
Completion of the Palm Springs Tennis Club Hotel and Palm Springs Public Library.

**1977**
June 27: Anna Cody dies in Palm Springs.

**1978**
August 29: Bill Cody dies in Palm Springs.

Cody office logo from his 1953 business card is used for the exhibit's poster.

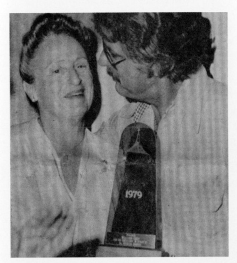

May 21,1979: Wini is presented with the Golden Palm Award by the Palm Springs Chamber of Commerce in Bill's honor for design excellence of St. Theresa Catholic Church. "Cody, who died last year, is considered by many as Palm Spring's most famous architect, who, in the words of one of his peers, spread the beauty of his architecture around the world." At the award luncheon, George Hasslein, praises Bill for his contribution to architecture and to his community.

July 1, 1981: Wini Cody dies in Palm Springs.

## 2004

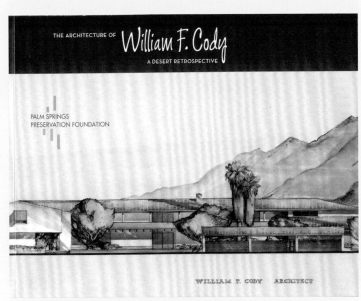

*The Architecture of William F. Cody: A Desert Retrospective,* cover design by Clara Nelson, published by the Palm Springs Preservation Foundation.

## 2010

Mayor Gordon Moller designates February 10 as the annual "William F. Cody Day" for the City of Rancho Mirage, California.

## 2012

February 17, 2012, during Modernism Week, the City of Palm Springs honors Bill with a sidewalk star on Baristo Road, adjacent to the Palm Springs Art Museum Architecture and Design Center and one block from the Del Marcos Hotel, his first internationally recognized commercial project. Jay Cody attends the event.

March 2: Jay Cody dies in Rancho Mirage.

## 2016

The exhibition *Fast Forward: The Architecture of William F. Cody* (July 10–October 2) opens at the Architecture and Design Museum, Los Angeles (A+D Museum). Organized and curated by Jo Lauria (then executive director of A+D Museum), Catherine Cody, Emily Bills, and Don Choi, the exhibition commemorates Bill's centennial birthday. Exhibition and banner design by Andrew Byrom.

## 2017

February 17–26, 2017, *Fast Forward: The Architecture of William F. Cody* opens at the Palm Springs Library to coincide with Palm Springs Modernism Week.

## 2021

Publication of *Master of the Midcentury: The Architecture of William F. Cody*, the first comprehensive monograph on the life and work of William F. Cody, coauthored by Catherine Cody, Jo Lauria, and Don Choi.

# William Cody's Artistic Development

Jo Lauria and Catherine Cody

The origins of artistic talent are often traced to family lineages; a family member of the older generation passes down the skills and knowledge to a younger member who demonstrates interest and aptitude for the subject. Consider the example of Anna Cody and her eldest son, William. From an early age, Bill revealed a natural talent for drawing and painting, and his mother encouraged and supported his artistic interests through directed instruction in the fine arts and the study of architecture. Anna was perfectly suited to mentor Bill; she was a graduate of the School of Applied Art in Philadelphia, an accomplished painter, and had worked professionally as an interior designer before marrying William Cody, Sr.

Eager to oversee Bill's art and architecture education, Anna provided her young son with illustrated books on the history of each, from which Bill drew copies of the buildings and their interiors to understand architectural structures and styles. Anna guided him in exercises to advance his skills of composition, proportion, perspective, and color theory. Anna's tutelage enabled Bill to acquire advanced drafting skills at an early age and engendered in him a sense of confidence and acute focus.

Anna also regularly took Bill on outings to sketch and paint landscapes and buildings *en plein air*, using these opportunities to teach him about the classical orders and the diverse styles of architecture, and coax him to identify these examples in the Los Angeles neighborhoods. When settling down to draw, Bill often set timed challenges for himself to complete a rendering of a building, developing his ability to rapidly transfer his observations to paper. Furthering his education of architecture, Bill traveled with his family throughout California visiting historic Spanish missions and haciendas. On family visits to relatives in the northeastern United States, Bill sketched and recorded buildings and points of interest.

Bill's creative talents were recognized and utilized outside of his household during his teen years. Bill served as the art editor and illustrator of his middle school yearbook. At Beverly Hills High (1931–34), he was selected as the illustrator for the school newspaper and designed stage sets for the performances of the drama department.

The affirmation Bill received for his drawing talents and Anna's reinforcement likely influenced his choice of architecture as a profession, and he calculated that his manual skills and design instincts would support his career choice. Like most architects in the pre-computer age, Bill was intensively trained in drafting and coloring, building on his home-taught experience. The era in which Bill came of age also had its influences. The mid-1920s to 40s was a period of discovery in the arts and sciences, and notably, technological advances in mechanical, electrical, and structural engineering thus providing the tools for design innovations. This had a profound effect on Bill as a young adult; later in life when designing for residential living he would strive to create a sensate atmosphere through indoor water features, controlled lighting, centralized fireplaces, and expansive views of nature through floor-to-ceiling sliding glass enclosures.

An early plein air pencil drawing of a Los Angeles residence on which Bill noted it took an hour and twenty-six minutes to complete; signed W.F.C.

An early plein air watercolor of a California mission.

An early plein air watercolor of a beach cottage, signed W.F. Cody.

Graphite and colored pencil drawing of a hacienda-style residence; USC class assignment, signed W.F. Cody.

Town Hall: a flattened arched arcade on the right and thin roof rotunda on the left again presage elements of the 1959 Palm Springs Spa entrance arcade. USC class assignment for Design II, signed W.F. Cody.

Bill's confidence in his robust foundational training prompted his acceptance at the University of Southern California College of Architecture and Fine Arts at the beginning of the winter semester, 1940; with degree he received from Santa Monica Junior College (now Santa Monica College) earlier that year, he entered USC as a sophomore. A review of drawings Bill executed while a student at USC demonstrates his progress in design and delineation. Drawings for his first-year design classes, such as *A Town Hall* and *Nautical Museum* (apparently assignments to imagine civic buildings) demonstrate his dramatic use of shading to articulate architectural volume, and attest to his command of space evidenced by the harmonizing of the built structure within its landscape. The second-year drawings *Memorial Library* and *A Night Club* express a refinement in composition, and also highlight Bill's understanding of the power of architecture to transform a site and determine the surrounding landscape. Fellow USC alumnus William Krisel commented on Bill's uncanny artistic skills: "When I entered USC, Bill Cody had graduated but was already a known and admired legend. His ability at watercolor perspectives was unequaled and shown [in class] as something that a true architect should master."

After graduating and obtaining his professional license, he remained committed to innovative approaches to architecture and the consistent incorporation of emerging technologies. Early in his career, Bill would learn that his masterful design and rendering skills were among his strongest professional assets, and the surest path to attract clients who were beguiled by his deft hand and design intellect.

An early pencil drawing of the interior of a gothic cathedral that Bill copied from a book, signed W.C.

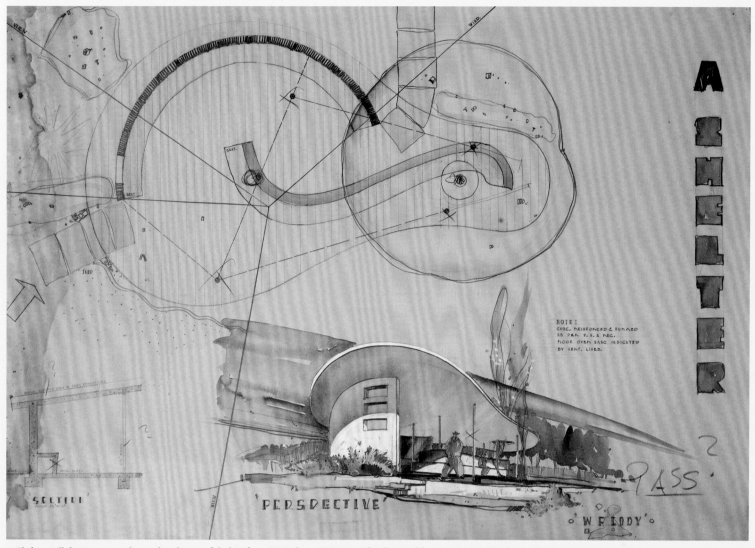

*A Shelter:* Bill designs an oculus in this thin roof shelter for a USC class assignment that he would incorporate in his design for the canopy of the Palm Springs Spa entrance arcade (1959), signed W.F. Cody.

Graphite, ink and white wax crayon rendering of *A School of Government*; USC class assignment for Design IV.

A graphite, ink, and colored pencil rendering of a multilevel residence; USC class assignment, signed William F. Cody.

*A Night Club*, colored pencil and watercolor. Structure to the right and hillside siting may be a possible reference to the Griffith Park Observatory; USC class assignment, signed William F. Cody Jr.

*Memorial Library:* entrance pierces a subtle horizontal curved façade, complementing the verticality of the building; USC class assignment, signed William F. Cody Jr.

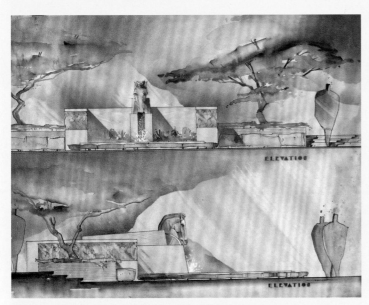

Ink and watercolor elevations of a fountain; USC class assignment.

*Beach Shelter* (watercolor, ink, and white wax crayon) dated October 16, 1940; USC class assignment for Design IV.

# William Cody's Early Work Before Licensure

Don Choi and Catherine Cody

William Cody's precocious talent attracted clients and employers long before he received his architectural license in May 1946. By that point, he had already worked for established engineering firms including Donald R. Warren Co. Engineers in Oakland and W.A. Bechtel Co. in Morenci, Arizona, as well as for celebrated designers such as W. Asa Hudson in Beverly Hills and Cliff May in Los Angeles. He had also designed award-winning schools as head designer for the Los Angeles firm Marsh Smith & Powell, Architects.

Cody's drive was apparent right out of high school, when he began working in architectural offices. He started with Heath Warton in 1935, a year after graduating, and the same year also started with Hudson, for whom he worked until entering college. He also opened a delineation and design service, working out of a room in his parents' house to produce drawings for builders and developers. Cody continued to work as an independent delineator and designer through his days at Santa Monica Junior College and then at the University of Southern California, amassing a rich portfolio of work for a wide range of clients while still in his twenties. His exceptional skills in graphite and watercolor allowed him to convincingly portray buildings across a range of types, running the gamut from rustic houses to colossal factories. This remarkably broad experience, along with his artistic talent, made him an unusually mature designer even before he opened his first design office at 11975 Santa Monica Boulevard in Los Angeles in 1944.

Among the many clients who commissioned drawings during Cody's early career Cliff May, played by far the largest role. When the two men first met, May was still in the early stages of developing the rambling, informal, low-slung residences soon to be widely known as ranch houses, and popularized by magazines such as *Sunset* and *House Beautiful*. Although often described as an architect, May in fact had no formal training and no architectural license, and relied on others to draw and develop his designs. In 1936, the year after May moved from San Diego to Los Angeles, Cody began producing drawings that helped May generate and express new perspectives on California houses and lifestyles.

During May's first years in Los Angeles, Cody produced drawings for several works crucial in establishing May's reputation, including the first Blow house, the Lily Pond house, and, most notably, the 36-acre Riviera Ranch development. Cody's expressive, romantic drawings served May's strategy of presenting buildings not simply as isolated objects but as expressions of contemporary life in California landscapes. For the Blow house, Cody crafted preliminary sketches as well as a perspective drawing of the final design, depicting buildings carefully placed in their natural settings. A presentation drawing for the Lily Pond house, a speculative home later known as the Mildred T. Boos house, shows a building whose white adobe brick walls, red tiled roof, and protected patio drew closely on May's fundamental affinity for historical California ranches. In the late 1930s, May's architecture remained relatively conservative in appearance even as he began to explore distinctive approaches to modern living.

For the Sunset Inn in Santa Monica, the Keith Apartment & Hotel Company commissioned this presentation drawing of renovations "as conceived by William F. Cody."

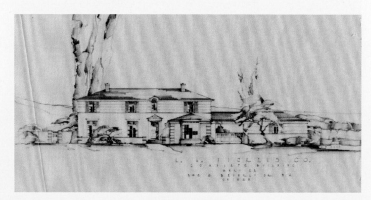

Cody produced several renderings of houses for the developer L.H. Pickens Co. of Beverly Hills.

The earliest known drawing Cody did for Cliff May is this delicate 1936 rendering of the Lieutenant Walker residence in San Diego.

Cody's study for the Blow estate gate shows his skill in inserting architecture into the landscape.

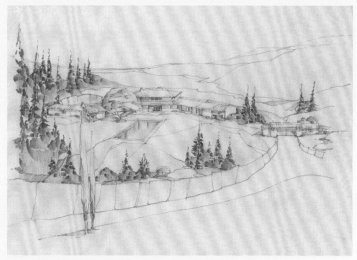

For the Westclox heir Frederic Blow and his wife, May and Cody created a rambling mansion in Mandeville Canyon.

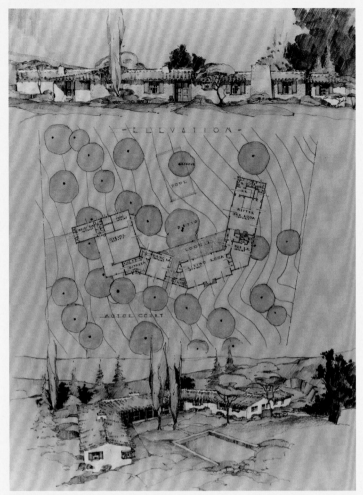

This presentation drawing of the Lily Pond house by Cody shows both the building plan and exterior views, a technique May and Cody often used to show both the architectural layout and the romance of the building in its landscape.

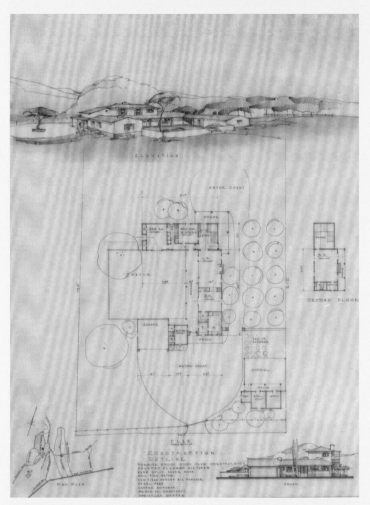

As drawn by Cody, the proposed Monterey Ranch residence for Riviera Ranch looked conventional in terms of layout and finish materials but also incorporated modern elements such as a gas forced-air furnace, at the time a very recent innovation.

Although the exact nature of the working relationship between Cody and May is unknown, it undoubtedly evolved as their architectural visions matured. At first, May probably saw Cody as a talented delineator rather than as a designer—at the end of 1936, Cody was only twenty years old and May twenty-eight. However, working for W. Asa Hudson, who designed many elegant Spanish Colonial Revival buildings as well as the iconic bungalows at the Beverly Hills Hotel, must have deepened Cody's knowledge of both historical California buildings and popular contemporary styles. Certainly he was familiar with the California Missions and with their uses of exterior spaces. As Cody gained more architectural expertise, he probably exerted more influence on May's designs as well.

May conceived the Riviera Ranch development in Los Angeles as a residential neighborhood with a strong identity created by a consistent architectural approach and a focus on equestrian activities. He designed and built all of the houses in the first stage of development at Riviera Ranch, including his own home in 1939; these residences served as model homes and provided the template for later buildings. Through deed restrictions, he ensured that all homes in the development would

be California ranch houses or in similar styles. Cody's drawing for a proposed "Monterey Ranch Residence" shows a typical layout: a low, one-room-deep, U-shaped building that presents a modest facade to the street and defines a spacious patio behind. As with other May houses, the construction mixed traditional elements, such as the hand-split wooden shake roof, with modern ones, for instance steel sash windows and concrete slab floor. As depicted by Cody, the communal stables were to resemble a California mission with whitewashed walls, tile roofs, deep porches, and an central patio. Given Cody's talent and his experience with the residential works of W. Asa Hudson, it does not seem unlikely that he assisted in designing the buildings of Riviera Ranch; however, since May did not publicly acknowledge any design role for Cody or other delineators, it is impossible to know for sure.

While attending USC from 1940–42, Cody continued to refine his residential design skills, and his USC portfolio includes projects that could have passed for work he did for Cliff May. However, his student work shows that he also began to investigate various types of modern architecture in depth. In 1941, he worked for W.A. Bechtel Co., a major engineering and contracting firm, as a designer and head draftsman for

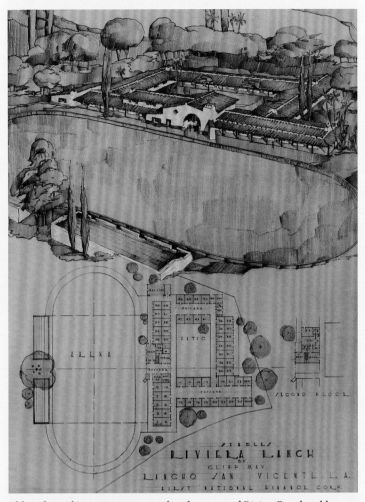

Although purely an equestrian complex, the proposed Riviera Ranch stables would have looked very much like a California Mission.

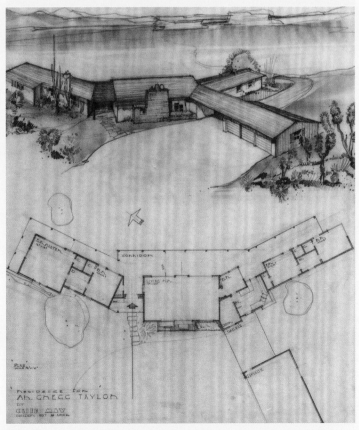

Although the rooms in the Taylor residence remain conventional boxes, the overall layout starts to resemble the centrifugal, pinwheel plans common to modernist buildings.

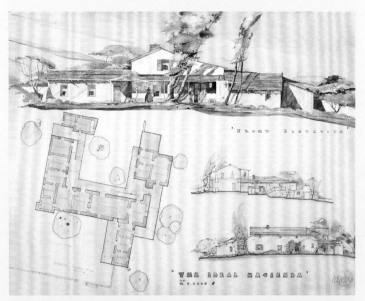

Planned as a one-room deep U around a courtyard, Cody's USC design for "The Ideal Hacienda" resembles houses such as the Monterey Ranch residence for Riviera Ranch.

This colossal factory for Kaiser Steel's new Fontana plant was one of several industrial buildings that Cody helped design for the war effort.

Labeled "William F. Cody Jr., architectural draftsman," this undated perspective drawing of a gas station combines modernist architecture with the quintessential Los Angeles building type.

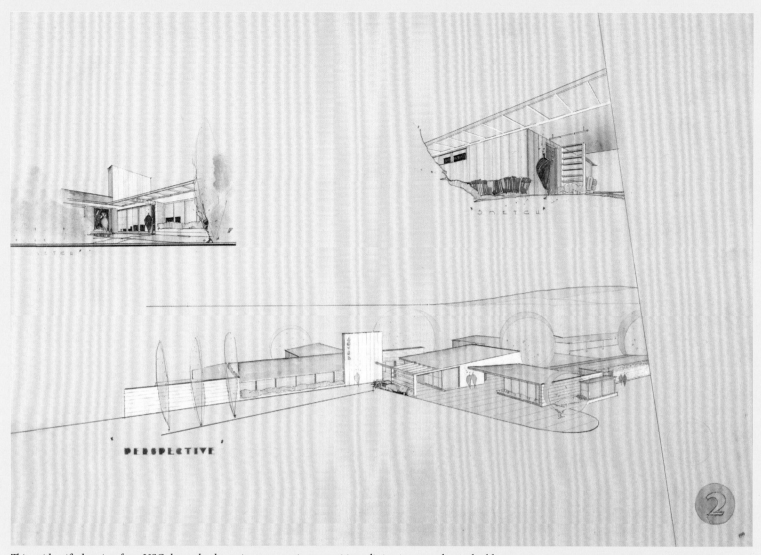

This unidentified project from USC shows the dynamic, asymmetric compositions distinctive to modernist buildings.

dormitories and school buildings in Arizona. In 1943, he gained the opportunity to work on cutting-edge industrial architecture, moving to Oakland after being commissioned by Donald R. Warren Company, Engineers to help design the new Kaiser Steel plant in Fontana, California. Part of the nation's large-scale wartime industrialization, this complex was the largest steel mill on the West Coast. Cody also did design and drafting for Blanchard Maher & Ward Architects of San Francisco on large-scale projects such as the Navy installation on Treasure Island. These projects certainly would have furthered his interest and expertise in steel construction, which he would later exploit to powerful effect for residential works, including his own house in Palm Springs.

Cody also continued to work with Cliff May, although less intensively given his employment with other architects and engineers. The modernist formal and spatial attributes Cody had explored while at USC—large glass areas, simple geometric forms, unadorned surfaces, and dynamic, asymmetric planning—happened to parallel certain characteristics of ranch houses. Certainly, May's deep appreciation for

California vernacular houses must have impressed Cody, while Cody's burgeoning modernist tendencies may have inspired May. Drawings from the early 1940s suggest that avant-garde ideas indeed began to play a larger role in May's work. Cody's evocative renderings of house designs for the actors Brian Aherne and Joan Fontaine depict thick walls and tile roofs but also free, asymmetric layouts perhaps indebted to modernist principles as well as to earlier May projects.

More explicitly modern yet was the Pace-Setter house, to which editor Elizabeth Gordon devoted the entire February 1948 issue of *House Beautiful*. Located in Riviera Ranch, this design grew out of May's Postwar Demonstration house, drawn by Cody in 1944, and expressed May's desire to update the ranch house for postwar living. Although clearly descended from May's ranch houses in terms of planning and outdoor spaces, the Pace-Setter house was more abstract, more elegant, and less rustic than his earlier designs. A contemporaneous residential design by Cody, though, shows that he adopted modernist spatial planning much more thoroughly than May had.

Cody's 1943 watercolor presentation drawing for the Indio, California residence of Brian Aherne and Joan Fontaine, who had won an Academy Award the previous year for Alfred Hitchcock's *Rebecca*.

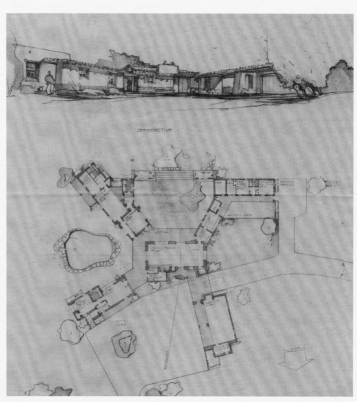

In this alternate version of the Aherne and Fontaine residence, the central courtyard is eschewed in favor of a sprawling layout that reaches out into the landscape.

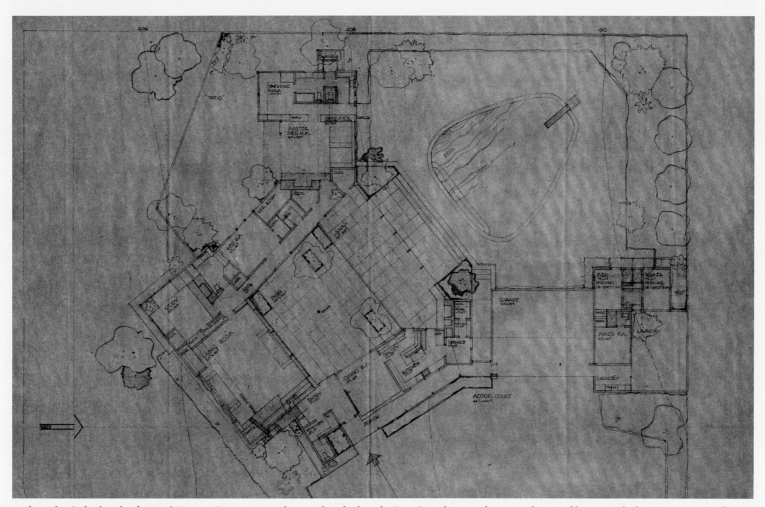

As drawn by Cody, this plan for May's Postwar Demonstration house—later built as the Pace-Setter house—shows a sophisticated layout in which rooms are oriented not only to a central patio, but also to the pool, the master bedroom patio, and other outdoor spaces.

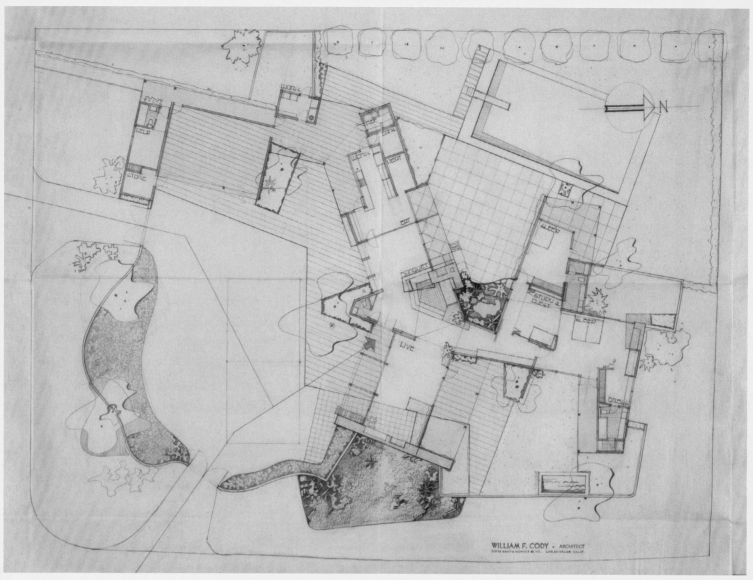

Compared with the Pace-Setter house, this unnamed design by Cody departs more thoroughly from conventional residential plans, notably in its free-flowing interior spaces and variety of angles.

While it is impossible to intuit precisely what May and Cody learned from each other, at the very least they shared a fundamental goal—to develop new modes of architecture that would serve as catalysts for the realization of truly modern California living. In the pursuit of this goal, they refined major themes over many years and projects, working together at first and then separately after the mid-1940s. They sought to unify interior and exterior spaces in the service of contemporary, informal lifestyles. They introduced modern technology into residences, for instance using radiant floor heating in works such as the Pace-Setter house and Cody's own residence in Palm Springs. They argued for enclaves in which consistent architectural principles were applied in the creation of distinctive individual houses, as seen at May's Riviera Ranch in Los Angeles and Cody's own Eldorado Country Club Estates in Indian Wells. Cody and May remained lifelong friends and the house that Cody designed for May in 1951 still stands on West Vista Chino in Palm Springs, a testament to their artistic affinities and mutual affection.

Cody's last major projects before licensure were the schools he designed while head designer for Marsh Smith & Powell, Architects from 1944 to 1946. Two of these works—Suva Elementary School and Corona del Mar Elementary School—garnered national awards from the American Institute of Architects. Cody's designs for Coachella Valley Union High School in 1945, along with his design for a church in Thermal the previous year, can be seen as a prologue to his remarkable career in the Coachella Valley. Although he kept his Los Angeles office until the mid 1950s, Cody moved to Palm Springs in 1946, finding success almost immediately with commissions such as the Del Marcos Apartment Hotel and the Dorothy Levin Residence.

This proposal for Coachella Valley Union High School is one of about a dozen school designs Cody worked on for Marsh, Smith & Powell.

Aerial perspective of the Coachella Valley Union High School proposal, dated November 1945.

# Awards and Recognition

**1944–46**
American Institute of Architects (AIA): First place national awards, Suva Elementary School and Corona del Mar Elementary Schools for March, Smith & Powell, Los Angeles (William F. Cody, head designer)

**1949**
AIA Southern California Chapter: Creditable Mention and Certificate of Honor, Del Marcos Hotel, Palm Springs.

**1962**
AIA (in cooperation with *House & Home* and *LIFE* magazines): Honorable Mention for design, W. & J. Sloane Co. Display House, La Quinta, California.

AIA, Honorable Mention for outstanding contribution to "Homes for Better Living."

**1963**
AIA Southern Chapter: Award of Merit, Robert and Betty Cannon Residence, Eldorado Country Club Estates, Indian Wells.

**1964**
AIA (in cooperation with *House & Home* and *The American Home* magazines):
Awards of Merit (for design), Cannon Residence and the J.B. Shamel Residence, Eldorado Country Club Estates, Palm Desert (Indian Wells), California.

American Institute of Steel Construction, Architectural Award of Excellence in recognition of outstanding aesthetic design: J.B. Shamel Residence.

The City Council, City of Palm Springs: award of distinguished service to the Council.

AIA 96th Annual Convention, St. Louis, MO: Reproductions of J.B. Shamel Residence on display.

AIA Homes for a Better Living program, featured in Award-Winning Houses: J.B. Shamel Residence.

**1965**
American Iron and Steel Award of Design Excellence in low-rise steel frame commercial construction (with Alfred N. Beadle and Laszlo E. Sandor of Dailey Associates): Western Savings and Loan Main Branch, Phoenix, Arizona.

City Council, City of Palm Springs: Distinguished Service Recognition as member of the Palm Springs Planning Commission from May 25, 1960 to March 26, 1965.

Inducted into the College of Fellows (FAIA) of the American Institute of Architects, Sheraton Park Hotel, Washington, DC: for "notable contribution to the advancement of the profession of architecture by his achievement in design." Cody's work is judged by its distinction, individuality, and mastery of the art of design.

American Institute of Steel Construction (AISC) Architectural Awards of Excellence: J. B. Shamel residence is one of eleven winners awarded on basis of "outstanding aesthetic design in steel." Winners were exhibited at the 1964/1965 New York World's Fair.

Palm Springs Planning Commission certificate of appreciation: "A Citizen of Distinction for Public Services by the People of the City of Palm Springs, Given Freely and Unselfishly on Section 14 Zoning Committee."

## 1966
Cody appointed vice president of the Inland California Chapter of the AIA.

Green and Clean Committee of the Valley Beautiful Citizens Council, Inc. Valley Beautification Award: for Western Savings & Loan Office, Tempe, Arizona.

## 1968
Cody appointed president of the Inland California Chapter of the AIA.

## 1969
Palm Springs Planning Commission, Desert Beautiful Outstanding Civic Award: for exceptional architectural beautification.

## 1973
AIA Inland California Chapter, Award of Excellence: Andreas Hills Condominiums, Phase II.

## 1974
Masonry Institute of the Inland Empire, Award of Merit: Tennis Club Hotel.

## 1979
Palm Springs Chamber of Commerce, Golden Palm Award of Excellence: for design of St. Theresa Catholic Church presented posthumously to Winifred Cody.

Annual "William Cody Award" established.

## 2010
February 10: Mayor Gordon Moller announces that February 10 is henceforward designated "William F. Cody Day" for the City of Rancho Mirage, California.

## 2012
*Palm Springs Walk of Stars* star awarded by the Architecture and Design Council of the Palm Springs Art Museum honoring William F. Cody sited adjacent to the Architecture and Design Museum.

## 2016
Architecture and Design Museum, Los Angeles presented the exhibition *Fast Forward: The Architecture of William F. Cody*, July 10 through October 3.

## 2017
Palm Springs Public Library presented the exhibition *Fast Forward: The Architecture of William F. Cody* during Modernism Week, February 17–26.

## Historic Preservation Designations

*City of Indian Wells Historic Preservation Society Site Designations:*
  Crank & Garland House #1, 1961

*City of Palm Springs Historic Site Preservation Board (HSPB) Site Designations:*
  Shell Service Station 2796 North Palm Canyon Drive, 1964

  Del Marcos Apartment Hotel, 1947

  James and Helen Abernathy Residence, 1963

  Racquet Club Cottages West designated Class One Historic District, 1960

*City of Rancho Mirage Historic Preservation Commission Site Designations:*
  John Gillin Residence, 1957

  The Fairway, 1969, the property private road was renamed Cody Court and classified as Class One Historic District

  Dr. Henry L. Jaffe and Mrs. Diana Gaines Residence, Tamarisk Country Club Estates, 1963

  Charles Jones Residence, 1957

  Barney Hinkle Residence, 1949

  Samuel and Gladys Rubinstein Residence, 1972

# Selected Bibliography

**Books and Other Media**

American Iron and Steel Institute. *Design in Steel 65*. New York: American Iron and Steel Institute, 1965.

Baker, Christopher P. *Palm Springs & Desert Resorts: A Complete Guide*. Woodstock, VT: Countryman Press, 2009.

Ballinger, Richard M., and Herman York, eds. *The Illustrated Guide to the Houses of America*. New York: Hawthorn Books, 1971.

Bell, Jonathan. "The Architects who built Palm Springs: William Cody." *Wallpaper, Architecture,* December 26, 2018.

Chavkin, Dan. *Unseen Midcentury Desert Modern*. Layton, UT: Gibbs Smith, 2016.

Coquelle, Aline. *Palm Springs Style*. New York: Assouline Publishing, 2005.

Cygelman, Adèle. *Arthur Elrod: Desert Modern Design*. Utah: Gibbs M. Smith Inc, 2019.

——. *Palm Springs Modern: Houses in the California Desert*. New York: Rizzoli, 1999.

Faibyshev, Dolly. *Palm Springs Mid-Century Modern*. Atglen, PA: Schiffer Publishing, 2010.

Gorst, Jake, dir. *Desert Utopia: Mid-Century Architecture in Palm Springs*. Denver: Design Onscreen, 2008, DVD, 58 min.

Harris, Frank, and Weston Bonenberger, eds. *A Guide to Contemporary Architecture in Southern California*. Los Angeles: Watling & Company, 1951.

Hess, Alan. *Forgotten Modern: California Houses 1940–1970*. Layton, UT: Gibbs Smith, 2007.

——. *Googie Redux: Ultramodern Roadside Architecture*. San Francisco: Chronicle Books, 2004.

Hess, Alan, and Andrew Danish. *Palm Springs Weekend: The Architecture and Design of a Midcentury Oasis*. San Francisco: Chronicle Books, 2001.

Heumann, Leslie, Teresa Grimes, and Peter Moruzzi. *City of Rancho Mirage: Historic Resources Survey*. Rancho Mirage, CA: City of Rancho Mirage, 2003.

Ino, Yuichi, and Shinji Koike, eds. *World's Contemporary Architecture*. Vol. 2, *U.S.A. (I)*. Tokyo: Shokokusha Publishing Co., 1953.

——. *World's Contemporary Architecture*. Vol. 4, *U.S.A. (II)*. Tokyo: Shokokusha Publishing Co., 1953.

Jansen, Charlotte. "Desert Modern Master: William F. Cody's original sketches go on display in LA." *Wallpaper, Architecture,* July 18, 2016.

Johns, Howard. *Palm Springs Confidential: Playground of the Stars!* Fort Lee, NJ: Barricade Books, 2004.

Lubell, Sam. *Mid-Century Modern Architecture Travel Guide: West Coast USA*. London, Phaidon Press, 2016.

Meeks, Carroll L. V. "Architecture" (in part). In *1950 Britannica Book of the Year*. Chicago: Encyclopædia Britannica, 1950.

Moruzzi, Peter. *Palm Springs Holiday: A Vintage Tour from Palm Springs to the Salton Sea*. Layton, UT: Gibbs Smith, 2009.

——. *Palm Springs Paradise: Vintage Photographs from America's Desert Playground*. Layton, UT: Gibbs Smith, 2015.

Niemann, Greg. *Palm Springs Legends: Creation of a Desert Oasis*. San Diego: Sunbelt Publications, 2006.

Ortner, Vyola J., and Diana C. du Pont. *You Can't Eat Dirt: Leading America's First All-Women Tribal Council and How We Changed Palm Springs*. Palm Springs, CA/Santa Barbara, CA: Fan Palm Research Project, 2011.

Riche, Melissa. *Mod Mirage: The Midcentury Architecture of Rancho Mirage*. Layton, UT: Gibbs Smith, 2018.

Rosa, Joseph. *A Constructed View: The Architectural Photography of Julius Shulman*. New York: Rizzoli, 1994.

Schnepf, James. *Palm Springs Modern Living*. Layton, UT: Gibbs Smith, 2015.

Serraino, Pierluigi. *Julius Shulman: Modernism Rediscovered*. Cologne: Taschen, 2017.

Shulman, Julius. *Architecture and Its Photography*. Edited by Peter Gössel. Cologne: Taschen, 1998.

Sotta, Andy, et al., Palm Springs Preservation Foundation. *The Architecture of William F. Cody: A Desert Retrospective*. Palm Springs, CA: Palm Springs Preservation Foundation, 2004.

Stathaki, Ellie. "Tour A Secret Palm Springs Modernist Icon, The Racquet Club Cottages West." *Wallpaper, Architecture,* February 11, 2020.

Stern, Michael, and Alan Hess. *Julius Shulman: Palm Springs*. New York: Rizzoli; Palm Springs, CA: Palm Springs Art Museum, 2008.

Street-Porter, Tim. *Palm Springs: A Modernist Paradise*. New York: Rizzoli, 2018.

University of Southern California. *El Rodeo* (yearbook). Los Angeles: Associated Students of the University of Southern California, 1940.

——. *El Rodeo* (yearbook). Los Angeles: Associated Students of the University of Southern California, 1941.

——. *El Rodeo* (yearbook). Los Angeles: Associated Students of the University of Southern California, 1942.

Von Eckhardt, Wolf, *Mid-Century Architecture of America*. Baltimore: John Hopkins Press, 1961.

Weiner, Stewart, ed. *The Desert Modernists: The Architects Who Envisioned Midcentury Modern Palm Springs*. Palm Springs, CA: Desert Publications, 2015.

Windeler, Robert. *Eldorado Country Club: Fifty Golden Years 1957–2007*. Indian Wells, CA: Eldorado Country Club, 2008.

——. *Thunderbird Country Club: 50th Anniversary History*. Rancho Mirage, CA: Thunderbird Country Club, 2002.

Zahn, Leo, dir. *Desert Maverick: The Singular Architecture of William F. Cody*. Studio City, CA: Picture Palace, 2016. DVD, 78 min.

Bill in his office, mid-1960s.

## Articles

"AIA Award Winner: A Sprawling Oasis in the Desert." *House & Home* 23, no. 2 (February 1963): 122–25.

"Airport Sketches Proposed Airport Administration Building." *Arizona Daily Sun*, March 11,1949, 1.

Anderson, Guy, "172 Prescott Drive … Smartest Address in Palm Springs." *Palm Springs Villager* (April 1952): 26.

"At the Golf Course at Palm Desert." *Architecture/West* 71, no. 11 (November 1965): 22–23.

Baird, Brittney, "Real Estate Home of the Month – Modern Manor." *Palm Springs Life* (January 30, 2015): 110.

Berges, Marshall. "Bob & Barbara McCulloch: The Inventive Manufacturer Turns His Ingenious Mind to Creating Gadgets for Fun and Convenience." *Los Angeles Times Home Magazine*, December 9, 1973, 78–80, 82.

*Beverly Hills Citizen*. "Former BH Architect Draws Plans for Palm Springs Spa." February 19, 1960, 8.

[Bill with his daughters]. *Palm Springs Villager*, July–August, 1953, 22.

Black, Kent. "Desert Dreamers 7: The Architects." *Palm Springs Life*, February 2018, 58–67.

Bowden, Caroline V. "Around the Neighborhoods: Quail Valley." *Fort Bend Independent* (Sugar Land, TX), October 10, 2012, 4.

Bradner, Liesl. "Palm Springs Style." *Los Angeles Times*, July 3, 2016, F2.

Brown, Renee. "The Visionary Architects Who Continue to Give Palm Springs Its Distinct Look." *Desert Sun* (Palm Springs, CA) (October 12, 2018): A29.

——. "William Cody Left Stylish Mark." *Desert Sun* (Palm Springs, CA), (February 21, 2015): A25.

Burden, Jean. "Modern with Mountains." *Los Angeles Times Home Magazine*, February 1, 1953, 33, 46.

"California-Spanish Model House." *Architectural Digest* 19, no. 1 (Spring 1962): 100–103.

"Cameron Center ... the Tomorrow of Palm Springs" (advertisement). *Palm Springs Villager* (February 1955): 26–27.

"Cameron Center ... the Tomorrow of Palm Springs" (advertisement). *Palm Springs Villager* 9, no. 9 (April 1955): 20.

"Cameron Center ... the Tomorrow of Palm Springs" (advertisement). *San Diego Magazine* 7, no. 5 (April–May 1955): 20–21.

Carlson, Edith. "Golf Course in the Front Yard." Desert Living. *Palm Springs Villager* 11, no. 10 (May 1957): 40–41.

[Cody L'Horizon Unit Drawing]. Robert C. Higgins, Building Contractor (advertisement). *Palm Springs Villager* November 1952, 6.

Colacello, Bob. "Palm Springs Weekends." *Vanity Fair*, no. 466 (June 1999): 192–211.

"Commercial Building by William F. Cody, Architect." *Arts & Architecture* 72, no. 9 (September 1955): 24–25, 35.

Copp, James. "L'Horizon Hotel." *Los Angeles Times* (Tuesday, January 12, 1954): 1 & 5.

"Covering the Campus: City Planning." *Southern California Alumni Review* 24, no. 2 (October 1942): 7.

Cracraft, Shar. "End-of-Season Events Go on at Palm Springs." *Press-Enterprise* (Riverside, CA), May 14, 1961, C-3.

"A Desert Caravansary ... Where Tennis Is King." *Masonry Industry*, April 1974, 2–3.

*Desert Sun* (Palm Springs, CA). "Aboard the SS Lurline." October 23, 1959, 7.

——. "Airport Terminal Study Continues." November 9, 1962, 3.

——. "Architect Cody Dies at 62." August 30, 1978, A2.

——. "Architect Elected as Fellow." June 10, 1965, 3.

——. "Architect William Cody's Home Built in 1952, Using Steel Sections." June 19, 1959, 6.

——. "Award Winner." February 1, 1974, B11.

——. "Blue Skies Trailer Village Latest in Modern Living." April 18, 1955, 3b.

——. "Cameron Center Bold in Design." July 1, 1960, 5.

——. "Checking Plans ..." December 2, 1955, 12.

——. "Club's 'Coming Out Party' Sunday." February 25, 1972, 18.

——. "Cody Appointed to Planning Unit." May 27, 1960.

——. "Cody to Inspect Mexican Style for Clubhouse." February 13, 1957, 4.

——. "Cody to Receive Award Tonight." June 7, 1949, 5.

——. "Cody Wins Award for Excellence." July 9, 1965, 7.

——. "Crosby, Benny, Hope Backing Trailer Park." April 29, 1954, 1.

——. "Dawson Outlines Program for 18-Hole Golf Course." April 7, 1950, 5.

——. "December 19, 1973, Cody receives second Award of Excellence for Andreas Hills, for Phase II, from the Inland Chapter of the A.I.A." February 4, 1974.

——. "Dedication Saturday." November 24, 1972, A3.

——. "Desert Living." August 4, 1950, 6.

——. "Design for Village Hotel Wins Prize for Architect." June 3, 1949, 6.

——. "Fidler's Home Attracts Throng." February 17, 1950, 4.

——. "For Cleaner Cars." November 8, 1954, 5A.

——. "Golden Palm Award Nominees Are Announced." May 11, 1979, C1.

——. "Ground Broken for Eldorado Clubhouse." January 21, 1959, 9A.

——. "Hotel de Marcos, Village's Newest, to Open March 5." February 24, 1948, 4.

——. "Hotel Has Grand Opening." October 10, 1973, A11.

——. "House of Tomorrow." April 2, 1948, 17.

——. "Initial Building to Be Started at Cameron Center." December 14, 1955, 1.

——. "'Lost' Cody house in Indian Wells dedicated." October 22, 2019, 1A & 10A.

——. "New Hotel Will Bring More Honors to Cody." October 1, 1973, D3, advertising supplement.

——. "New Style Shops Go Up at Palm Desert." October 24, 1947, 21.

——. "Northend Gas Station's Coming." August 9, 1963, 1.

——. "Opening of Spa Set for Jan. 12." December 21, 1959, 1A, 10B.

——. "P.D. Sign Dedication Due." May 17, 1968, 3.

——. "Pure Luxury." December 19, 1972, E13.

——. "Ready for Monte Carlo." December 30, 1959, 3.

——. "Recognition." April 26, 1974, C7.

——. "Royal Palm Gallery Newest Local Project." March 24, 1950, 7.

——. "Something New." September 1, 1950, 2.

——. "The Springs to Make Formal Debut Friday." December 19, 1956, 1.

——. "St. Theresa Church Construction Begins." April 22, 1967, 18.

——. "St. Theresa's Receives 2 Architectural Awards." May 22, 1979, A1.

——. "Three Tram Tower Sites O.K., Report." November 16, 1948, 1.

——. "Thunderbird De Luxe Trailer Park Planned." April 19, 1954, 2B.

——. "Valley War Dead Due Honor on Memorial." August 8, 1968, 4.

——. [Walt Disney Home]. December 20, 1951, 14.

——. "William Cody Given Award for PD Home." May 15, 1964, 16.

——. "Workmen Swarm Sunset Towers in Completion Job." June 19, 1952, 1.

——. "Woolworth's in Cameron Center." May 21, 1960, 1.

"Designer's Desert Home." *Architectural Digest* 25, no. 3 (Winter 1968/69): 88–93.

"Design for Vacation Living." *Architectural Digest* 27, no. 4 (January/February 1971): 44–55.

Downs, Maggie. "Desert Dreamers." *Palm Springs Life*, May 2017, 42–47.

[Eldorado Country Club]. *House and Home* (June 1964): 98.

[Entrance Sign for the City of Palm Desert]. *Palm Desert Post* (September 15, 1966).

"Environment Controls Design." *Architectural Record* 107, no. 2 (February 1950): 85–89.

"Environment Impact Report, 2016." Campus Master Plan, California State University, San Bernardino (July 2017): 63.

"Familiar Buildings Win A.I.S.C. Awards." *Architectural Record* 138, no. 4 (October 1965): 346.

"Fast Forward: The Architecture of William F. Cody." *SAH/SCC News* (Society of Architectural Historians/Southern California Chapter) Presidents Letter. July/August 2016, 3.

Feltman, Charles H. & Jean. *The American Home*, June 1952, 110–11.

Fong, Dominique. "Historic Home Model for Area Country Clubs." *Desert Sun* (Palm Springs, CA), March 28, 2014, A25.

Gallishaw, Phil. "Cody, after Nine Years Here, Has Projects in Mexico, Cuba." *Desert Sun* (Palm Springs, CA), December 2, 1955, 12.

"Golfers Attention!" *Palm Springs Villager* (May 1952): 31.

Graves, Pauline. "Open Plan." *Los Angeles Times Home Magazine*, March 6, 1966, 31.

Greer, Gloria. "Play Is the Thing." *Palm Springs Life*, July 1962, 26–34.

Gringeri-Brown, Michelle. "Just Deserts." *Atomic Ranch*, Spring 2013, 36–44.

"Ground Breaking Ceremony …" *Palm Springs Life*, *Desert Living Edition* (August 1962): 20.

Gueft, Olga. "Contract Giant: Parvin/Dohrmann Company." *Interiors* 123, no. 7 (February 1964): 97–99.

"Haines' Headquarters: Ex Movie Star Designs an Uninhibited Studio." *Interiors & Industrial Design* 109, no. 5 (December 1949): 72–79.

Hart, Lisa Marie. "Desert Prophet." *Palm Springs Life*, August 2016, 26–37.

Hotel de Vacances a Palm Springs [illustrations, plans] (French), U.S.A. V.15, No. 147–148, 1954: 36–37.

*Houston Post*. "Houstonians Live in Desert Style." September 18, 1960, section 7, 1.

Hyland, Dick. "Valley Wide Shopping Center." *Palm Desert Post* (Palm Desert, CA), June 18, 1964, 1.

*Independent-Journal* (San Rafael, CA). "You May Get Wet at New Golf Course." September 7, 1957, 7.

"Inland Celebrates Chapter Charter Installs Officers." *Southwest Builder and Contractor* 147, no. 8 (February 25, 1966): 29.

"Institute's Awards Point Up Variety in Use of Steel." *New York Times,* February 7, 1965, R1-8.

Jarmusch, Ann. "Desert Modern." *San Diego Union-Tribune*, November 5, 2006, I-18.

Koush, Ben. "Westward Ho: Remembering the Robinson House." *Cite: The Architecture & Design Review of Houston*, no. 80 (Fall 2009): 36–39.

[L'Horizon Hotel]. *Desert Magazine* (Palm Springs, CA) (January 2007): 65.

Lopez, Frank G., ed. "Building Types Study No. 151 … Building for Athletics and Recreation: Projects: High School Gymnasium, Flagstaff, Ariz." *Architectural Record* 106, no. 1 (July 1949): 133.

Lorraine. "Nicoletti Home Looks Out Over Desert and Golf Courses." *Press-Enterprise* (Riverside, CA), May 14, 1961, B-5, B-11, B-12.

*Los Angeles Examiner.* "AIA Honors 6 Southland Architects." June 12, 1949, 25, News-Feature section.

*Los Angeles Times.* "Awards Made to Architects." June 12, 1949, part V, 1.

———. "Cantonese Restaurant Set for Palm Springs." December 6, 1959, part VI, 15.

———. "Club Completed at Palm Springs." March 22, 1953, part V, 14.

———. "Expansion Program at Spa Completed." November 12, 1961, J23.

———. "Fraternity Dwelling Being Readied at SC." December 8, 1957, part VI, 1, 3.

———. "Indian Land Leased in Palm Springs Area." February 16, 1958, part VI, 1, 4.

———. "Luxury Hotel to Adjoin Resort City Health Spa." April 15, 1962, J10.

———. "Palm Springs Spa to Be First Desert High-Rise." November 14, 1965, J30.

———. "Spa Hotel to Stay Open Year Around." April 1, 1973, part X, 8.

———. "Tennis Club Homes Rising." April 4, 1965, J26.

———. "$2 Million Mineral Wells Project Near Completion." December 20, 1959, part VI, 5.

———. "Work Advanced on New Hotel." April 26, 1953, part V, 4.

*Los Angeles Times Home Magazine.* "Balanced Power Homes" (advertisement). June 25, 1961, 32–33.

———. "Entrances That Reach Out to Meet You." October 15, 1967, 76–77.

———. "In the Desert, A Mood of Mexico." May 6, 1962, 36–37.

———. "Personality Is the Mark of a Successful Kitchen." February 27, 1966, 18–21.

Lotz, Jan. "Tennis' Silver Anniversary on the Desert." *Palm Springs Life Desert Living Issue*, June/July 1960: 15.

"Louise Nicoletti's 'Little Eldorado'–Showplace in the Desert." *Palm Springs Life, 1961–62 Annual Pictorial*, September 1961, 58–65.

"Luxury Living on Wheels." *Palm Springs Life*, Annual Pictorial, 1960, 88.

MacMasters, Dan. "The Magic Is in the Blending." *Los Angeles Times Home Magazine*, April 23, 1967, 18–23.

———. "This Desert Home Meets All Requirements." *Los Angeles Times Home Magazine*, December 1, 1963, 16–19.

Marsh, Smith & Powell Architects and Engineers. "Desert Chapel, Thermal, California." *Architectural Record* (September 1945): 95.

Mendoza, Mariecar. "William Cody to Get Next Star on Walk." *Desert Sun* (Palm Springs, CA), February 15, 2012, [14].

Merchell, Tony. "William F. Cody, Our Least-Celebrated Modernist, May Have Been the Most Influential." *Palm Springs Life, At Home Desert Living*, October 2001, 7–9, 62.

"The Mission Valley Dream." *San Diego Magazine* 8, no. 6 (January 1955): cover, 20–24, 34, 36–38.

"Modern Times: Renewed Horizons." *Modernism* 10, no. 1 (Spring 2007): 35.

Morton, Carol E. "[Tribute to Russell Wade]." *Highway 111*, Summer 2006.

[Mr. & Mrs. Kay Karahadian Residence (HOAMS Construction Co., Inc.) (advertisement)]. *Palm Springs Life,* (September 1958): 52.

Murbarger, Neil. "Lois Kellogg of Fools Folly." *Palm Springs Villager* (April 1954): 18.

Murphy, Rosalie. "Exploring St. Theresa, Palm Springs' Modernist Church." *Desert Sun* (Palm Springs, CA), (February 3, 2016): A25.

Nelson, George. "The House in the Desert." *Holiday* 13, no. 3 (March 1953): 60–63, 135–36.

"A New 18 Hole All-Grass Golf Course for Palm Springs" (advertisement). *Palm Springs Villager*, 4, no. 10 (May–June 1950): 4.

"New Hotel: Elegance and Luxury." *Tennis Club Nettings* 11, no. 10 (September 1973): n.p.

"New Mortuary Planned Here." *Arizona Republic* (24, April 1950): 13.

*New York Times.* "Art Accessories Move from Homes into Club." January 26, 1960, 28.

"1964 Award Winners." *House & Home* 26, no. 4 (October 1964): 69–79.

Oliver, Pat Phillips. "The House with the Look of Forever." *Palm Springs Life,* December 1968, 56–58.

"One of the New Desert Miracles: The Pleasure Places." *Vogue (*May 1961): 170–75.

"A Paradise for Golfers." *Palm Springs Villager* (April 1953): 18–19.

"A Paradise for Golfers: Tamarisk Country Club." *Palm Springs Villager* (November 1952): 20.

"Pavilion in an Oasis." *Interiors* 123, no. 6 (January 1964): 66–70.

Perrault, Mike. "Snapping Up the Sweet Life." *Desert Sun* (Palm Springs, CA), November 26, 2012: 1.

Pinkston, Mary Anne. "Structure Is The Design." *Desert Magazine*, October 2004: 72–77.

Pricer, Jamie Lee. "Fashion Show a Family Tradition." *Desert Sun* (Palm Springs, CA), November 30, 2009, B3.

"The Racquet Club; Movie Colony Hideaway." *Palm Springs Life, 1960–61 Annual Pictorial* (September 1960): 46.

"Recipe for a Workable Kitchen." *Sunset* 113, no. 6 (December 1954): 56–59.

"Residence of Mr. and Mrs. Earle M. Jorgensen, Thunderbird Country Club, Palm Springs, California." *Architectural Digest* 15, no. 1 [1958]: 10–16.

"Residence of Mr. and Mrs. W. A. Moncrief, Palm Springs, California." *Architectural Digest* 16, no. 3 [1959]: 108–12.

"Resort Hotels." *Architectural Forum* 91, no. 1 (July 1949): 94–106.

Riche, Melissa. "Thoroughly Modern Cody." *R/M: The Magazine of Rancho Mirage* (2020): 50–59.

Ringwald, George. "Many-Angled Restaurant Building to Open Friday after Year's Work." *Daily Enterprise* (Riverside, CA), December 18, 1956, Desert and Pass edition, B1.

Roth, Alfred. "Amerikanische Kleinhotels." *Werk*, no. 6 (1951): 162–71.

Salkin, Judith. "Architects Collaborated on Spa Project." *Desert Sun* (Palm Springs, CA), February 26, 2011, [49].

———. "Cool Home, A Midcentury Standout." *The Arizona Republic*, July 30, 2011: HO1-O2.

"Selected Details: Motel: Cantilevered Porch." *Progressive Architecture* 32, no. 9 (September 1951): 115.

Sells, Helen. "Good Housekeeping's Portfolio of 101 Decorating Ideas: Today's Living Rooms." *Good Housekeeping* 129, no. 5 (November 1949): 50–53.

[Shamel Residence Foyer Pool Image]. *Perfect Home Magazine*, (July 1980): 8.

Shess, Thomas. "Palm Springs Pied-à-Terre." *San Diego Magazine* 54, no. 2 (December 2001): 120–25.

"Shopping Center by William F. Cody, Architect." *Arts & Architecture* 72, no. 10 (October 1955): 18–19.

"Sixteen Southern California Architects Exhibit Contemporary Trends in a Group Showing at Scripps College." *Arts & Architecture* 67, no. 4 (April 1950): 22–33.

"Some Plain, Some Fancy." *Palm Springs Villager* (April 1952): 43.

Sorvetti, Laura. "Desert Modern: The William F. Cody Papers." *Cal Poly*, Spring/Summer 2016, 13.

[Southern California Chapter of the American Institute of Architects Honor Award Dinner]. *Fortnight* 6, no. 13 (June 24, 1949): 15.

*Southern Cross* (San Diego). "New Church Slated in Palm Springs." March 3, 1966, 1.

"Tamarisk Country Club Opens." *Palm Springs Villager* (December 1953): 22.

Taylor, J. M. F. (Bud). "Crusade Against Mediocrity: A Profile of William F. Cody, A.I.A." *Palm Springs Life, 1960–61 Annual Pictorial*, September 1960, 69–96.

———. "Russell Wade in Never Look Back." *Palm Springs Life, Desert Living Issue*, October 1960, 67–72.

———. "William F. Cody A.I.A., A Comment on Architecture" *Palm Springs Life, Desert Living Issue*, August 1964, 26–33.

Thorpe, Harriet. "What to see at Modernism Week in Palm Springs." *Wallpaper, Architecture* (February 2020).

"Thunderbird Country Club Opening." *Palm Springs Villager* (May-June 1950): 4.

Wade, Russell. (advertisement) "Thunderbird Home Offered … Louise Nicoletti Residence for Sale." *Palm Springs Life* (August 1965), 42.

Weigel, Fred C. "$1,000,000 Eldorado Clubhouse Approved: December Start Planned for 'Golfer's Golf Course.'" *Desert Sun* (Palm Springs, CA), November 21, 1958, 1.

"William F. Cody, Desert area architect, will be honored …" *Palm Springs Life* (June 1965): 13.

Winship, Sian. "Special Collections." *SAH/SCC News* (Society of Architectural Historians/Southern California Chapter) Presidents Letter. May/June 2015, 2.

# Acknowledgments

*To my husband, Ricardo Nemirovsky, to my family, and in loving memory of my father, Bill Cody.*
**Cathy Cody**

*To my family and especially my supportive husband, Michael, who has shared this long journey.*
**Jo Lauria**

*To the families Choi and Kuhn-Choi, most of all to my wife Devin.*
**Don Choi**

We are most grateful to our publisher Monacelli, and editorial director Alan Rapp, who had the vision and fortitude to accept and refine our manuscript for publication, exercising patience and summoning encouragement at critical junctures.

Thanks to Wim de Wit for crucially positioning William F. Cody within the context of progressive twentieth-century architecture. Andrew Byrom, whose collaboration extends back to his exhibition design of *Fast Forward,* brought his familiarity with and sensitivity to the vast trove of Cody's personal and professional materials to create an inspired publication that will be an asset on any bookshelf. Consulting editor Greg Dobie was instrumental in the book's early development, assisting in shaping the concept and fleshing out its bibliography.

We are beholden to the contributors of the exhibition *Fast Forward: The Architecture of William F. Cody* at the Architecture and Design Museum: Tibbie Dunbar, Emily Bills, Andrew Byrom, Erin Kasimow, exhibition design; Olson Visual, graphic sponsor; Eder Cetina, creative consultant; Katie Whorrall, exhibition project manager; and Toby Tannenbaum and Iryna Stein, education and programming.

Our sincere appreciation goes to the Special Collections and Archives at Kennedy Library, California Polytechnic State University, San Luis Obispo, especially director Jessica Holada and department specialist Laura Sorvetti, to whom we are indebted for their help accessing the William F. Cody Papers many times over many years. We also thank the Special Collections team, including archivist Berlin Loa, digital repository coordinator Michelle Wyngard, digital archivist Zach Vowell, and Ross White of the GIS Cody mapping project.

The capable hands of Aimee Lind and Ted Walbye of the Getty Research Institute provided additional archival assistance and steered us through the process of obtaining reproduction rights from the Getty Foundation.

Thanks as well go to Emily Chung, Gabrielle Icardo, and Amanda Radner, Dr. Don Choi's students at Cal Poly, who spent many hours searching through the William F. Cody Papers to assist with research.

Our gratitude extends to the board of the Palm Springs Preservation Foundation for their educational and programming support for Cody's works in Palm Springs, especially to president of the board Gary Johns and treasurer Barbara Marshall, who facilitated the publishing partnership between the foundation and Monacelli. Special thanks also to Steven Price for introducing this project to PSPF, and to vice president Steven Keylon for guiding it through the review process—and to both for conferring their enthusiastic endorsement.

To my sister Lynne (Cody) Brady, our heartfelt thanks for sharing her fond childhood memories and photographs that have further enriched the story of our father and family. We are also grateful to our generous friends and hosts who provided accommodations for the book's research and development in California and Arizona: Tom and Gayl Biondi, La Quinta; Jonathan Clough and Paul Murphy, Palm Springs; Dene Collins, San Diego; Tracey Hasslein, Northridge; Jessica Holada, San Luis Obispo; Patricia Hulbert, San Diego; Jan and David Lansing, Palm Springs; Janice and Tom Marohn, Scottsdale; Don Pattison, Palm Springs; Ruta and Ed Saliklis, San Luis Obispo; Sandy and Bill Sanders, Cathedral City; Jilda and Peter Schwartz, Palm Springs; Randy and Lisa Stromsoe, Templeton; Adrienne Turner, Chula Vista.

Numerous individuals allowed access to William F. Cody structures, provided research assistance, shared materials and stories, and otherwise encouraged our work. We are grateful to each of them, as this publication is a result of their assistance: Sheldon & Stephanie Anderson; Ray Corliss; Vince and Linda Dwan; Allison Engel; Don Flood; Barbara Foster-Henderson; Claudia Foster; David and Laura Goone; Michael Johnston and David Zippel; Carol Saindon Kerfoot; Alexandra Lavie; Lemurian Fellowship members; Piper Mavis; Mrs. Milbank McFie; Jessy Moss and Steve Jocz; Paula Petrie; Dr. Gary Price; Gladys Rubinstein; Stephen E. Sessa; Ann and Tom Warde.

We are immensely grateful to all the photographers whose stunning images grace this publication. The photographers who provided contemporary photographs include Francisco Nuñez Alfaro, FNA Tours; Darren Bradley; James Butchart; Dan Chavkin; Don Choi; Mark Cieslikowski; Philip Dagort; Douglas Fisher; Don Flood; David Glomb; David S. Goone; James Haefner; Patrick Ketchum; Kelly Peak; Jim Riche.

**Additional support includes:**

**Research and Materials**
David Bricker; Lauren Weiss Bricker; Tracy Conrad; Adèle Cygelman; Frank Jones; Andre Kim; Lucile Lac; Julia Larson; Frank Lopez; Patrick McGrew; Clara Nelson; Mia Picerno; Melissa Riche; Julie Rogers; the Sinatra Family Archive; Colby Tarsitano; Kelly O'Day Wade; Leo Zahn.

**Family, Friends, and Colleagues**
Wanda Barton; John (Jay) Cody and family; George Hasslein; Henry Hester; Ira Johnson; A. Quincy Jones and Elaine Jones; Roger Jones; Hugh Kaptur; William Krisel; Richard Le Duc; Terry Masters; Robert Messmer; Carol Morton; Paul Neel; James Ritter; Ned Sawyer; Morris Skenderian; John Vogley.

**Libraries and Historical and Preservation Societies/Foundations**
Bob Berg, Rancho Mirage Historic Preservation Commission; Renee Brown, Palm Springs Historical Society; David Bryant, Rancho Mirage City Library; Jeannie Kays, Palm Springs Central Library; Raymond Keller, Rancho Mirage Historic Preservation Commission; Rob Pitchford and Luke Leuschner, Historical Society of Palm Desert; Celeste Reyes, Riverside Public Library; Adele Ruxton, Indian Wells Historic Preservation Foundation; Jeri Vogelsang, Palm Springs Historical Society; Julie Warren, Palm Springs Central Library.

**Project Support and Encouragement**
Paul Bockhorst; Robert Broms; Mark Davis; Sally Dempsey; Amanda Erlinger; Kitty Kiley Hayes; Alan Hess; Doug Ireland; Patricia Kaplan; Steve Keylon; William Kopelk; Steve Maleski; Sharon Mills; Katie Nartonis; Jade Thomas Nelson; Courtney and Joy Newman; J.R. Roberts; Don Van Dijk; Lisa Vossler Smith; Kim and Joe Zakowski.

# Contributors

**Catherine Cody Nemirovsky** is the third daughter of William and Winifred Cody. With a background in residential building design and interior design, she became steward of her father's papers in 2006, and began preparing a biography. As part of her research, Cody Nemirovsky cocurated the exhibition *Fast Forward*, celebrating William Cody's centennial with organizing curator Jo Lauria, professor of architecture Don Choi, and architectural historian Emily Bills at the Architecture and Design Museum in 2016.

**Jo Lauria** is a Los Angeles-based curator, writer, and educator. She received her curatorial training at Los Angeles County Museum of Art, and is a specialist in the fields of design and craft whose research explores objects and architectural environments that define American lifestyle and culture. Lauria has organized significant touring exhibitions and published extensively, receiving the American Ceramic Circle Book Award for *Ralph Bacerra: Exquisite Beauty* in 2016. She is Mentor Faculty at Otis College of Art and Design and Adjunct Curator of American Museum of Ceramic Art.

**Don Choi** is an architectural historian who specializes in modern Japan and California. He holds an AB in economics from Princeton University, a MArch. from Rice University, and a PhD. in architectural history from the University of California, Berkeley. He conducted his doctoral research under Dr. Terunobu Fujimori at Tokyo University's Institute of Industrial Science. Currently he is professor of architecture at California Polytechnic State University, where he teaches courses in architectural history and theory.

**Wim de Wit** is an architectural historian and independent curator of architecture and design. He has worked as a curator of architectural collections at various institutions in the Netherlands and the United States. Between 1993 and 2013, he worked at the Getty Research Institute in Los Angeles, first as Head of Special Collections and Curator of Architecture, and then as Head of the Department of Architecture and Contemporary Art. He is currently preparing a book about twentieth-century Los Angeles architect Welton Becket.

# Image Credits

Unless otherwise credited, the reproductions in this book are courtesy of the William F. Cody Papers and William F. Cody Papers 2, Special Collections and Archives, Robert E. Kennedy Library, California Polytechnic State University, San Luis Obispo.

Rob Adams: 159–61

© 2014 Francisco Nuñez Alfaro, FNA Photo Tours: 229–30, 231 bottom, 232, 233 bottom, 234–35

Darren Bradley: 11 top right, 201–07, 209–10, 215, 217 bottom left and right, 218–19

James Butchart: front cover, 143–45

Dan Chavkin: 15 top left, 254 third row left, 255 top right and second row left, 257 top right

Don Choi: 15 bottom right, 21 top right, 24 top right, 25, 28 bottom right, 220 bottom left and right, 221 bottom left

Marc Cieslikowski: 185, 226 top left and bottom, 227, 239, 244 top, 259 middle left, 285 top right

Zeni T. Cieslikowski Sr.: 50 bottom, 100

Catherine Cody: 96, 97 bottom left and right, 211 top, 212 bottom right, 220 top, 221 top

Winifred A. Cody: 267 top left, bottom left, and middle, 268 left, 269 top right, 272 top right, 273 bottom right

Phil Dagort: 157 bottom, 284 top right, 290 bottom, 258 top right

George de Gennaro: 73, 75–77

Jerry Duchscherer: 189–91

Eldorado Country Club promo sheet: 100

Farnsworth House: 28 top right

Doug Fisher: 45, 47 top left and right

Don Flood: 263 bottom right, 265 bottom

*The Desert Sun*: 285 top left

Getty Images, The Life Picture Collection, photo by John Dominis: 65 bottom

© David Glomb: 180 top, 181, 183 top

Google Earth: 213 bottom: Image 2020 Landsat / Copernicus. 238 top: Image 2019 Landsat / Copernicus.

David Goone: 196–99

James Haefner: 153–56, 259 middle right

William Haines Designs: 46 top left and right

Marian Henderson Collection, Historical Society of Palm Desert: 261 second row right and bottom left

Mel Jones: 133 bottom left and right

Patrick Ketchum: 255 top left

Erwin Lang: 83–84, 85 top and bottom left, 86 bottom, 87–89, 113

Jo Lauria: 15 top right, 47 bottom

Lemurian Fellowship: 211 bottom, 212 left and top right, 213 top

McBride & Keller: 70 bottom right

Leo McDonald: 269 top left

Patrick McGrew: 253 bottom right

David M. Mills, photographer (postcard published by Ferris H. Scott): 94 bottom

Don Milton: 275 bottom left

Nickerson-Samuelson-Kaye Advertising: 268 top right

Paul Oxley-Maxwell Studio: 68 bottom, 69, 70 bottom left

Palm Springs Art Museum, Leland Y. Lee: 261 second row left

Courtesy of Palm Springs Historical Society: 51 top left and bottom, 65 top (photo by Ray Jones), 85 bottom right, 187 bottom right, 244 bottom, 245 bottom left, 258 top left, 277 bottom left

Courtesy of Palm Springs Life Archives: 92, 110 bottom, 122, 126, 127 bottom left and right, 179, 180 bottom, 183 bottom

Palm Springs Public Library: 245 bottom right

Kelly Peak: 118 top left, 120 top and bottom

Photographer Unknown: 62 top, 95 bottom, 102 bottom (courtesy Carol Morton), 117, 148, 150 top, 151, 174 bottom left, 186, 187 top and bottom left, 195, 221 bottom right, 222–23, 256, 257 top left, 259 bottom right, 261 top right, 267 top and bottom right, and middle left, 269 bottom left and right, 270, 271, 272 top left and bottom, 273 top and bottom left, 303

Paul Pospesil: 240 top

QA Architectural Arts: 112 top

Jim Riche: 233 top, 255 third row left, 259 bottom left

Charles Schneider, *Palm Springs Life* December 1968: 263 top right

Courtesy of Sheldon and Stephanie Anderson: 258 bottom right

Julius Shulman photography archive © J. Paul Getty Trust, Getty Research Institute, Los Angeles (2004.R.10): front jacket and back cover, 13, 14, 20, 26 top right and bottom left, 27 top left, 28 left, 29 top left and right, 30 top left, 35, 36 top, 37, 39–43, 46 bottom right, 61, 62 bottom, 63 top and bottom, 93, 97 top, 99, 103–07, 109, 111 bottom, 112 bottom, 114–15, 137, 138 bottom, 139–41, 163–65, 167 top and bottom right, 168–69, 171–73, 174 top and bottom right, 175–77, 251 second row left, 253 top and middle right

Gail B. Thompson, Gayle's Studio (courtesy Tracy Conrad): 53, 55 bottom, 56–57, 59 top right, 67, 68 top, 70 top right and left, 71, 93, 97 top, 131, 132, 133 top, 134, 149, 150 bottom, 267 middle right

*Thunderbird Country Club* magazine 1953: 51 top right

Cal Turner, *The Desert Sun*: 242

UC, Santa Barbara, Cliff May Papers, Architecture and Design Collection; Art, Design & Architecture Museum: 293 second and third row left and right, 294, 295 left column, 297 top right

Harold Waltz: 110 middle